GOOD GIRL

a memoir of overcoming
rape, breast cancer
& fundamentalism

Laura Jensen Walker

Published in association with The Lab Publishers

Good Girl: A Memoir of Overcoming Rape, Breast Cancer, and Fundamentalism

Laura Jensen Walker

Published by

Laura Jensen Walker

in association with

The Lab Publishers

Print ISBN: 979-8-9859407-0-1

Ebook ISBN: 979-8-9859407-1-8

First paperback edition 2022

Cover by Erin Dozois

Edits by Kate MacGregor

Interior formatting by Ben Wolf, Inc. (www.benwolf.com/editing-services)

Excerpt from *Thanks for the Mammogram!* by Laura Jensen Walker, copyright © 2020 Used by permission of Revell, a division of Baker Publishing Group.

CONTENTS

PRAISE FOR GOOD GIRL

"GOOD GIRL is that rare find—a memoir of tough times that is neither harrowing nor saccharine but rather brutally honest, sharply intelligent, courageous, clear-sighted, and even funny. Yes, you will boil with sympathetic rage, but the smooth-as-silk writing turns every page into a pleasure and Laura Walker's indomitable spirit will make you stand up and cheer."

—Catriona McPherson, multi-award-winning author of *In Place of Fear* and the bestselling Dandy Gilver series

"Loved it! My hand was on my heart as I read. This is the best, most honest writing Laura Jensen Walker has ever done."

—Annette Smith, bestselling author of *Whispers of Angels*

"Anne Lamott meets Erma Bombeck...Laura Jensen Walker's page-turning story is an amazing combination of inspiring, hilarious, and heartwarming. Walker's unlikely journey from 'good girl' to self-actualized adult...drove her into a life of secrets and searching. In her dramatic and deeply affecting memoir, she guides the reader through her lifelong transformation from self-blame to emotional freedom. If you are ready to laugh and cry by turns, to find yourself inspired and motivated, this book is for you."

—The Reverend Jane A. Willan, Senior Pastor of First Church West Hartford and author of the Sister Agatha and Father Selwyn Mystery series

"A marvelous book! A mix of funny, snarky, poignant, self-deprecating, and deadly serious when it needs to be. What a journey Laura Walker has had. It was a privilege to get to read in depth about the pivotal experiences of her life—written so beautifully."

—Becky Johnson, bestselling author/co-author of more than sixty books including *We Laugh, We Cry, We Cook*

"A disarmingly honest look at what happens when an intelligent, thoughtful, and free-spirited young woman is sexually violated. It is a powerful, insightful, and beautiful coming-of-age story (yes, in our sixties) that reveals the *ordinariness* of how we absorb, adapt, and respond to exploitation over time—until we can reclaim our worth. Ms. Walker is a gifted storyteller, and this book is a stirring example of transcendence."

—Maria Vidos Hunt, PhD, retired psychotherapist and Director, WeMe Mindfulness

"Laura Walker's memoir gives us a reminder that resilience is possible, even in the face of violence, illness, and institutional toxicity. She takes us on a journey of bravery and courage as she confronts being raped and challenges the abusive culture of religious fundamentalism. It is a story of perseverance that will bring hope to many."

—The Reverend Debra Warwick-Sabino, Rector, The Episcopal Church of our Saviour

"Laura Jensen Walker has seen a thing or two and has lived not only to tell the tale but has done so with grace, humor, compassion and wisdom. Especially for all us gals who have taken some time to live beyond the acceptable margins of religion and rightness. A gift."

—Lisa Samson, author

For Lonnie Hull DuPont with much love and gratitude.
Thanks for encouraging me to go deeper.

And in memory of my beloved parents, David and Bettie Jensen,
and brothers, Todd and Tim, who left us way too soon.

Secrets, silent, stony sit in the dark palaces of both our hearts: secrets weary of their tyranny: tyrants willing to be dethroned.
—James Joyce, *Ulysses*

I've never read *Ulysses* (and let's face it, never will) but the quote above eloquently illustrates my story and is literary and deep, so I'll take it.

Author's Note

Out of respect for their privacy, I have changed the names of some of the people in these pages. It is my story, not theirs.

Also, memory ebbs and flows with age, so although certain memories remain diamond-sharp after many years—firmly embedded in my consciousness, as much as I might wish them not to be—others are fuzzier. Some details have faded over time, yet I share these remembrances as best as this sixty-something brain can recall.

GOOD GIRLS AND THE-THING-THAT-MUST-NOT-BE-NAMED

A girl should be two things: who and what she wants.
—Coco Chanel

I've always been a good girl.

Growing up in the 1960s, I was a polite, straight-A student who respected her elders, went to church on Sunday, and never gave her parents any trouble.

As a teen in the seventies, I didn't drink, swear, do drugs, or sleep around. I was the poster child for good girls everywhere.

Until that night.

It was my fault. I was asking for it. Good girls born in the 1950s and raised on Doris Day movies and MGM musicals know better than to wear short skirts, tight jeans, or snug tops.

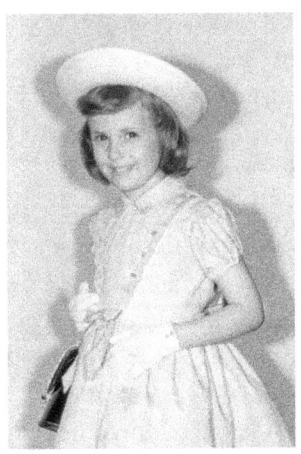

In my Easter bonnet.

And they certainly know not to go into a bar alone.

I wasn't alone initially. My midwestern girlfriend, who I was visiting from Phoenix, took me to her college hangout that snowy winter's night, a week before I left for Air Force basic training. She introduced me to her friends clustered around the noisy bar, who in turn introduced me to rum-and-cokes and tequila shots.

Once my friend's boyfriend arrived, the two of them left to go make out in a dark corner while I, a nerdy nineteen-year-old wallflower unaccustomed to male attention or drinking, continued doing shots with the cool college kids, including a hot fraternity jock named "Tom."

Soon I was falling-down drunk. "I should prolly go home," I said, my speech slurred. Dizzy and stumbling, I looked around for my girlfriend.

"They left," frat boy Tom said, steadying me. "Do you need a ride to her dorm? I can take you."

"Really? Thanks." *And my mother said chivalry was dead.*

I stumbled through the snow, shivering in the cold, my thin Arizona shoes slipping and sliding on the Wisconsin ice, the chivalrous Tom in heavy boots keeping his arm tight around me as he led me to the parking lot. Once inside his car, he turned on the heater, which made me even sleepier. Then he French-kissed me. *Me.* The girl who never went to prom or homecoming. I nodded off and passed out.

When I came to, there was a strange man on top of me.

Loud music and male laughter pierced my fuzzy, alcoholic haze. My head lolled to one side. I squinted and could just make out some brawny jock types lined up drinking beer, clapping chauffeur Tom on the back, giving him something (money?), and leering at me.

I couldn't breathe.

Crushed beneath that heavy male weight, I instantly sobered up. Terror does that. I was trapped in a strange room, in a strange city, with strange men. Big. Strong. Drunken. Men. Men who didn't know me from Eve. And no one knew I was there.

No one.

Newspaper accounts of the raped and naked bodies of young women found in the woods flashed through my head. If I protested, what would they do? Beat me? Cut me? Strangle me? Who would ever know? I was alone and at their mercy.

A conversation I'd had a few years earlier with my new stepfather came back to me. He had asked in a casual, sex-education tone what I would do if I ever found myself in a situation where it was a question of saving my virtue or my life. Which would I choose?

"My virtue," I proudly replied in all my righteous sixteen-year-old virginity. Chastity was the most important thing a good girl possessed. Growing up, that truth had been drilled into me. Good girls waited until the wedding night. Otherwise, they were "spoiled" or "damaged goods" no decent man would want. TV shows and movies I watched as a tween, like *Peyton Place* and *Where the Boys Are* (with Connie Francis and that great sixties song), reinforced this immutable truth.

My dispassionate stepfather set me straight. "Your life is more important than your virginity. It's just sex."

Recalling those words and not wanting to lose my life, I kept my eyes shut during the frat boys' male bonding ritual. I pretended to still be passed out as I ran away in my head.

Far, far away.

It's just sex, I told myself, and I had already had sex. It's not like I was a virgin. I did not date in high school—no boy ever asked me out—but I did read Erica Jong's *Fear of Flying* and Gloria Steinem's new, groundbreaking *Ms.* magazine, which taught my burgeoning feminist self that women had as much right as men to have sex. *I* was in charge of my own sexuality. As a result, I experimented a little.

It's just sex, I told myself again in that midwestern college fraternity house as the frat boys took turns and I continued to run away in my head. Sex couldn't hurt me.

Only it did.

Little did I know how much that night would color the rest of my life. I vowed to myself then that no man would ever have control over me again.

Eventually, chauffeur Tom drove me back to my friend's dorm as I kept my eyes shut in the passenger seat, pretending to be asleep. I didn't tell my girlfriend what had happened. I didn't tell anyone. Even myself. For a long time.

Years later in counseling, I learned that women who have been sexually assaulted or molested often respond in one of two ways: they either shy away from sex and intimate relationships altogether or become hyper-sexualized and promiscuous. For years, I did both. I didn't question what I was doing or examine it. Instead, I jumped headlong into sex, after first locking away into the deepest corners of my psyche the-thing-that-must-not-be-named.

It would be more than forty years before I truly examined the impact of that night in the fraternity room.

I was a Wonder Bread girl scout raised in Wisconsin on fried-Spam sandwiches, Miracle Whip, and Lay's potato chips. Not an official Girl Scout with the green uniform and cool badges —too expensive for our struggling family of six—but the girl scout with good manners and good grades, who always followed the rules, said, "Yes, sir. No, ma'am," and answered the phone, "Jensen residence, Laura speaking." (Which set the stage for my becoming a killer secretary when I grew up.)

Don't hate me, but I was one of those teacher's pets who won spelling bees, received the most gold stars for reading 103 books in Miss Vopelensky's first-grade class, and got straight

A's until fifth-grade math came along and ruined my record. Math has not been my friend ever since second grade when those pesky fractions went and stood on top of each other.

I was a textbook girl scout for much of my life, but at twenty-eight, when my conservative fundamentalist fiancé wanted to give me a sewing machine as a wedding present, I knew I wasn't going to make it as a good Christian wife.

"I don't sew," I told him. "Not since seventh-grade Home Ec, when I sewed Kathy Hansen's finger to my muumuu. I was so traumatized I haven't worn a muumuu since."

It's true. The garment's ugly factor had nothing to do with it.

"Every woman should sew," my fiancé insisted. "My mom made all my sisters' clothes when they were growing up. It's much cheaper than store-bought."

I wonder if his mother had sewn his clothes if he'd have felt the same way. And then I wish I'd kicked his sorry-ass self to the curb. Truth is, he dumped me one week before the wedding. My first epic fail as a good Christian girl.

2
GOOD GIRL BEGINNINGS

I like adventures and I'm going to find them.
—Jo in *Little Women* (Louisa May Alcott)

My first good-girl fail came at seven.

On Sundays, Mom usually took my sister Lisa and me to Holy Communion Lutheran Church, a beautiful, tall church set on a hill in our small town of Racine, Wisconsin. Whenever Mom was working a Sunday shift at her waitress job, my great aunt and uncle took us to their church instead: a boxy, one-story, nondenominational, "holy-roller" church as my non-churchgoing father called it. Not as pretty as the high church on the hill with the gorgeous stained glass, but a lot more fun, with Jesus flannel graphs and clap-happy songs.

Aunt Dorothy and Uncle Bill were our rich relations. At least that's what it seemed like to my seven-year-old eyes, accustomed to living in a series of rentals with Salvation Army furniture, hand-me-downs, and regular helpings of Dinty Moore beef stew and my mom's version of Hamburger Helper pre its actual invention (fried hamburger, canned Franco-American spaghetti, and Niblets corn all mixed together). Aunt

Dorothy, Uncle Bill, and Great-Grandma Jensen lived in a gorgeous white house they *owned* over in a nice part of town.

We never owned a home. A mortgage was a luxury afforded solely to the rich.

Inside Aunt Dorothy and Uncle Bill's house, I admired the elegant celery-green walls, white-shuttered French doors, and the wood-burning fireplace with delicate china figurines I wasn't allowed to touch on the mantel. They even had a piano like *The Lawrence Welk Show*, except theirs had a crystal candy dish on top.

That candy dish was always full of an unending supply of chocolate—namely, Hershey's miniatures. My favorite was the plain milk chocolate, but often when we visited, the only kind remaining were nasty Mr. Goodbars. Despising nuts, yet a rabid chocoholic, I would discreetly nibble away at the chocolatey goodness surrounding the peanuts. Then I'd suck each nut clean of every trace of chocolate and store them in the side of my mouth like a hamster. (The same way I did with peas, the despised green vegetable that squished when I bit into it.) I would then politely excuse myself to go to the bathroom where I would spit out the hated nuts into the wastebasket and cover my sin with a tissue.

When I returned to the living room, my sister and I would perform for the grown-ups. Kindly Grandma Jensen with her beatific countenance, sweet disposition, and cloud of snowy white hair would beam at us and tap her foot as we sang such American classics as "Harrigan" from Dad's favorite musical, *Yankee Doodle Dandy*, and "Winston tastes good like a cigarette should…"

Devout churchgoers, Aunt Dorothy and Uncle Bill sponsored Lisa and me to attend Bible camp in the Wisconsin woods. At camp, we enjoyed swimming, nature walks, arts and crafts, making s'mores, singing "Kumbaya" around the campfire, and girl-crushing on cabin counselor Debbie.

Debbie was the most gorgeous teenager I'd ever seen—a cross between Annette Funicello and Audrey Hepburn in *Sabrina*. With glossy brown hair pulled back into a high ponytail that bounced when she walked, she could have been a Breck girl.

Breck was *the* shampoo of the fifties, sixties, and early seventies. With their long, lustrous hair, Breck girls were the standard of feminine beauty. Christie Brinkley, Farrah Fawcett, and Jaclyn Smith—the latter two who would shoot to fame in *Charlie's Angels*—were all Breck girls. I yearned to be a Breck girl and shake my shiny cascading chestnut curls in reckless abandon, but my mousy brown hair and the "cute" pixie haircut my mom always made me get thwarted those longings.

The ubiquitous pixie cut fresh from swimming.

Debbie was not only beautiful; she was also good. Wherever Debbie went in her sleeveless buttoned-up blouses, knee-length shorts, and white Keds, she glowed with goodness.

Everyone loved her. All the girls wanted to be her. All the boys, particularly the male counselors, wanted to marry her.

The girls in our cabin fought for her attention. "Debbie, would you braid my hair? Debbie, would you help me with my memory verse?" Meanwhile, I followed Debbie-the-good around like a cocker spaniel, lapping up everything she said and waiting for that Jesus-y goodness glow to rub off on me.

The only glow I got was from standing too close to the campfire toasting marshmallows.

In our cabin that smelled of pine, Bazooka bubble gum, and wet rubber bathing caps, the other girls giggled as they braided each other's hair.

"I'm going to marry a doctor when I grow up and live in a big house with lots of rooms for our six kids," said golden-haired Cindy. "And he'll bring me roses every day."

"I'm going to marry a banker so we'll have lots of money and he can take me to Niagara Falls on our honeymoon," said Patty, who reminded me of Pocahontas, whom we had recently learned about in school, with her waterfall of long black hair. "And I'm going to have two boys and two girls, so the boys can take care of their sisters."

"Well, I'm going to marry a minister and have as many children as my husband wants," said sweet, strawberry-blonde Sally.

"How many kids do you want, Laura?"

"Huh?" I lifted my pixie-head from my latest Trixie Belden adventure. I identified with the hardscrabble tomboy Trixie and liked her better than girly Nancy Drew with her fancy convertible, who always had to use her rich father's name to help her out of scrapes. Trixie, the thirteen-year-old detective who lived on a farm with her parents and brothers, did chores like me and didn't run to adults when she had a problem—she solved it herself, or with the help of her friends. And, like me, Trixie wasn't good at math.

"How many children do you want when you get married?"

"I'm not getting married," I mumbled around a mouthful of Cracker Jack. "I'm going to become a writer and write lots of books and travel all over the world."

The long-haired cabin girls looked at me as if I had horns growing out of my head. Devil horns. The dream of every churchgoing, Easy-Bake-Oven-playing little girl in the 1960s was getting married and having kids: the pinnacle of good-girl happiness.

Each day at Bible camp, we would learn new stories about heroes of the faith, like Moses, David, and Noah. David was my favorite because he was little and scrawny like me yet took out the giant Goliath with only a slingshot. We didn't hear many stories about women, except for Mary, the mother of Jesus; bad-girl Mary Magdalene; and Eve, who disobeyed God in the Garden of Eden and is the reason sin came into the world. We would also memorize the verse of the day and sing songs with lots of clapping and fun hand motions.

I loved the singing. It made me feel all warm and good inside.

Each night, the camp director would ask who had memorized the daily Scripture. At the end of camp, the two who had memorized the most verses were presented with a New Testament—a small white one with an embossed gold cross on the cover for the girl and a sturdy black one for the boy. I coveted that little white New Testament with everything in my converted sinner being but lost out by two verses to a goody two-shoes whose name I've long since forgotten, but I'm pretty sure ended in 'y.'

On the bus home from camp, Lisa and I sang along lustily with the other kids—complete with hand motions. "I've got the joy, joy, joy, joy, down in my heart, down in my heart, down in my heart. I've got the joy, joy, joy, joy, down in my heart, down in my heart to stay."

That joyful song died on our lips the minute we climbed into our old green Rambler in the church parking lot. Mom and Dad had been fighting again, or as they called it, "having a discussion." When Dad tried to pick back up the "discussion" our arrival had interrupted, Mom hissed, "Not here! Wait until we're away from church." Then she turned and offered a bright smile and waved out the passenger window to our neighbors picking up their kids.

Mom and Dad had many discussions, usually about money and our lack thereof, and Mom did most of the discussing. She could swear like a sailor, but only within the confines of our home. Before I was out of kindergarten, Mom had broadened my vocabulary with a litany of blue language. But the first, and only, time I used one of those words, she washed my mouth out with Zest.

I would have preferred her pink bar of Camay.

Mom had a jealous streak too. She was especially envious of my dad's younger sister and her husband who worked at two of the main factories in our midwestern town. "I used to *babysit* her!" she would yell. "And now she owns her own house while we rent an upstairs flat!" (My parents fell for each other after Dad came home from the Navy and met the pretty, seventeen-year-old babysitter taking care of his younger siblings.)

Dad had tried working in the factory alongside all his blue-collar friends and relatives, but as a dreamer and artist with an artist's sensibilities, he just couldn't do it. "There's more to life than sitting and pulling a lever all day long," Dad told Lisa and me as he painted canvases in the basement. He quoted Thoreau: "If a man does not keep pace with his companions, perhaps it is because he hears a different drummer. Let him step to the music which he hears, however measured or far away."

My different-drummer dad worked various jobs as a printer, sign painter, and salesman. He had a huge vocabulary and could sell anything to anyone. Dad, who nicknamed me *Yenta Mi*—Danish for *my little girl*—was the smartest, most talented man I knew. I hung on his every word.

My father dropped out of high school at seventeen to join the Navy and see the world, but he was a voracious reader and a self-taught man, forever learning new things and eager to impart his knowledge to his four offspring. He would bring home copies of *Life* and *National Geographic* to show us there was a bigger world out there beyond our small factory town.

Like Henry Fonda's character in *Spencer's Mountain*, the 1960s film precursor to *The Waltons*, my father was never much of a churchgoer. Dad believed in God and the Golden Rule of doing unto others as you would have them do unto you, but he didn't have much use for, "the hypocrisy of people in church who act holier-than-thou on Sunday and lie, gossip, and treat others, especially the poor, like dirt the rest of the week." Yet he and Mom made sure we went to Sunday school and said our nightly prayers.

My sister Lisa, fifteen months older than me, would kneel beside me at our matching twin beds as we scrunched our eyes shut and prayed, "Now I lay me down to sleep, I pray the Lord my soul to keep. If I should die before I wake, I pray the Lord my soul to take."

Saying the *die* part scared me, but my parents reassured me that people didn't usually die until they were old. And taking my soul just meant I'd live forever in heaven where the streets were made of gold, and I would have everything I needed and wanted—including Mr. Goodbars minus the nuts. We would end the death prayer by asking God to bless Mommy, Daddy, our friends and relatives, and all the starving children in Africa, China, and India.

Where Dad was smart and talented, Mom was the prettiest, classiest mother on the block. Except for that whole swearing and rage thing.

My mother believed and lived out the adage "Cleanliness is next to godliness" by keeping an immaculate house and enlisting my sister and me early on to help maintain that home perfection. Mom and her six sisters, known as the "Miller Girls," were raised by their mother, my Grandma Miller, to be queens of clean. Mom continued that clean tradition with Lisa and me.

Every Saturday we dusted, vacuumed, and scrubbed to the strains of Mantovani, Mitch Miller, and my personal favorite, Doris Day. *Que sera, sera.* Mom delegated the task of rinsing out my younger brothers' dirty diapers (pre-Pampers) in the toilet to my sister and me. Lisa, being older, always grabbed the Number One diapers and stuck me with the dumpy, fragrant Number Twos.

Jensen Family, circa 1962 (I'm on the left.)

As a kid, I wasn't that close to my mother. To my young eyes, she seemed obsessed with cleaning, appearances, money

—which we never had—and stuff. For months Mom saved up tips from her waitressing job to buy an elegant white couch that was her pride and joy. Then she kept that couch covered in plastic (years before Ray's mom in *Everybody Loves Raymond*) so my siblings and I wouldn't dirty it with our grubby hands or spill Kool-Aid on it. The thick plastic slipcover stuck to our bare legs, and we had to peel our thighs slowly from it inch-by-inch or risk painful leg-skin annihilation. In the humid Wisconsin summers, in our non-air-conditioned house, it became our own personal slip and slide. No water needed, just add sweat.

I preferred hanging out with my dreamer dad, who introduced me to art, Mario Lanza, classic old movies, and books. Dad also drilled us nightly at the dinner table on the "It Pays to Increase Your Word Power" section of *Reader's Digest*.

Growing up, I read constantly. (Still do.) Reading opened new worlds to me, far away from Mom's rages and the endless succession of rentals in our Wisconsin town. By the time I was thirteen, we had moved more than a dozen times. I was always sneaking off somewhere to read. Often up a tree.

Mom always found my secret hideaways. "Laura Jean, get your nose out of that damn book and come do these dishes," she'd yell.

Mom was slender yet curvy, with a tiny waist ("36-22-36," she and Dad would proudly tell us), and she wore her shoulder-length brown hair up in an elegant French twist for work, or on the rare occasion when my folks could afford to go out on a date. In the mid-sixties, she got a short, stylish Sassoon cut and dyed her hair jet black, which complemented her Cleopatra-style eyeliner from Avon.

I loved watching my mother put on her makeup, especially lipstick. I would sprawl on the end of my parents' bed (no Lucy and Ricky Ricardo twin beds for *my* parents), chin propped in my grubby tomboy hands, and stare, mesmerized, as she sat in front of her mirror and carefully applied Platinum Rose or Love That Red from Avon to her perfect Elizabeth Taylor lips.

Mom would form the top half of a heart on her upper lip first, swipe a thick stripe across her bottom lip—left to right and back again—and end by smacking a kiss onto a tissue to blot off the excess. If we were out of tissue, she used the nearest piece of paper at hand, occasionally tearing off a lined sheet from my black-marbled school composition notebook.

Grabbing those discarded papers, I would match the kiss mark against my own lips as practice for the day when I would be old enough to wear lipstick and cause men to whistle. Which they always did when my pretty mother walked down the street, hips swaying.

Mom had a way of catching men's eyes. One pair of eyes my mother caught was her boss's. During that time, the "discussions" between my parents grew more frequent. As a result, the summer after my high school freshman year, my folks packed us up to move to Phoenix, the valley of the scorching sun, where Mom's family lived.

If we had known it would be the death of my dad, we never would have moved.

3

DUST TO DUST IN THE DESERT

The death of a beloved is an amputation.
—C. S. Lewis

I hate Phoenix. The dusty desert, the ugly cactuses masquerading as landscape, the scorpions, and the unrelenting heat that sizzled at 113 degrees, burned my hand when I opened the car door, and kept my pasty Scandinavian skin captive inside a house that had nothing but an old, rusty swamp cooler for air conditioning.

Mostly I hate Phoenix because it killed my father.

Our fresh start out West when I was fourteen found Dad working three jobs to pay the rent: a dry cleaners by day, a janitorial service with Mom by night, and selling eyeglass repair stuff on the side.

It was too much for my father's slight midwestern body, accustomed to four seasons, especially in that blistering Arizona heat. Dad wound up in the emergency room with chest pains, which the doctor initially thought were indigestion.

Not indigestion. A heart attack. Before the age of forty.

Three weeks after the hospital released Dad, he was home recuperating, and late one night he was working on his painting of Paris's Arc de Triomphe. I sat next to him, watching one of the old black-and-white movies we loved on TV. Lisa had fallen asleep on the couch, Mom wasn't home from their janitorial job yet, and my younger brothers, Todd and Tim, were asleep in their room.

Suddenly, Dad dropped his paintbrush and grabbed his chest. "I feel sick," he said, staggering into the kitchen and heaving into the sink.

Only nothing came out.

He kept retching, and I tried to give him some water but he couldn't drink. He groaned from the pain.

"Daddy!" I screamed.

Lisa woke up and came running in just as Mom got home from work. Mom raced into the kitchen and called Uncle Jimmy, a highway patrol officer and all we had in those pre-911 emergency days.

"I think Dave's having another heart attack," she yelled into the phone as I supported Dad at the sink. "What do I do?"

Mom dropped the receiver. "I need to take your dad to the hospital. Uncle Jimmy will meet us there. He's calling ahead to alert the ER."

Daddy. Daddy. Daddy. Please be okay, Daddy. Please be okay, Daddy.

"I want to go with you."

"No, you girls need to stay here and watch your brothers."

I helped Mom get Dad to the car with Lisa following close behind, talking to him the entire way. "It's going to be okay, Daddy. You're going to be okay." Once we got him in the car, Dad's head lolled back over the top of the seat and his eyes closed.

"I love you, Daddy," Lisa and I said in unison, holding his

hands through the passenger window, the tears streaming down our cheeks.

He squeezed our hands—the special family signal for *I love you* that he had taught us when we were little—and gasped out, "Take care of your brothers."

Then Mom sped off into the night, and my sister and I went back inside and prayed. We prayed and prayed, but the prayers didn't work. My father died that December night in 1971 at thirty-eight years old.

Before my first date. First kiss. And first byline in the school newspaper.

A couple months before Dad passed away, my sixteen-year-old sister had gotten involved in the 1970s Jesus People movement that was sweeping the country. Lisa was always playing something called Maranatha music on the record player in our shared cinder-block bedroom. She had also started wearing shapeless prairie-style dresses that covered her from neck to ankle, Jesus sandals, and no makeup.

One morning as I was getting ready for school, Lisa looked over the top of her John Lennon glasses at me as she clutched her Bible to her calico-clad breast and pronounced, "You're going to hell for wearing short skirts and red lipstick."

"At least I know I'll look good there."

After Dad died, my sister became even more involved with her weird Jesus-people group, becoming president of the Christian club on our high school campus and lugging her Bible everywhere. Even to class. Talk about embarrassing.

Mom started taking us to Lisa's church after we lost Dad, but it was all a little too hippie-ish and huggy for me. Total strangers would give me a wide and goofy grin, grab me in a bear hug, and say, "Jesus loves you." As someone who needs her personal space, I wanted to wipe those sappy smiles right off their faces by punching them in their Dunkin' Donut Christian bellies and shouting, "Get your hands off me!" But yelling wasn't allowed in church.

The church people kept talking about reaching the lost, saying the only way to heaven was if you said the "sinner's prayer" and asked Jesus into your heart. I'd had my ticket to heaven stamped when I went forward as a kid at Bible camp when I was seven, but what about my dad?

The dad who never went to church.

Where was *he*? What if he hadn't said the sinner's prayer? Was he lost for all eternity? Would I never see him again? Was he burning in hell? Was he stuck in some kind of cosmic limbo or purgatory somewhere? Where *was* he?

The thought that I might never see my beloved father again was too horrible to imagine. Yet I did imagine it. I had nightmares about it.

One afternoon when I was sobbing on my bed, consumed by grief and desperately missing my father, I cried out to the golden-hued picture of Jesus that always hung over our canopied double bed.

"Where is my daddy? Where *is* he?" I fell into an exhausted sleep and awakened to see my dad standing at the foot of the bed, smiling down at me, eyes brimming with love.

"Daddy!" I cried, reaching for him in my still half-asleep state.

A wavy image of Jesus smiling down at me, eyes brimming with love, replaced the image of my father. And I knew my daddy, my father, was safe in heaven.

Throughout childhood, I was a fearless, skinny tomboy who climbed trees, played Tonka trucks with Jeff Willis across the street, made intricate snow forts with my younger brothers, beat the boys at school in foot races, and rode my electric-blue Schwinn through the neighborhood hands-free.

When my dad died, I lost some of that fearlessness and began gaining weight. I've struggled with my weight ever since. At birth, I was an itty-bitty thing, weighing only five pounds, thirteen ounces. I was never one of those cute chubby babies with dimpled thighs that adults cooed over and found irresistible.

I have the dimpled thighs now, but they're not irresistible.

At nineteen, a couple days before I enlisted in the Air Force, I weighed one-hundred-and-forty-four pounds, three pounds over the max weight allowed for my age and height of five-foot-seven. On enlistment day when I weighed in, if the scales registered one-hundred-and-forty-four, Uncle Sam would not let me in.

Desperate, I ate hardly anything the day before. Chicken bouillon and a few grapes. That night I popped a diuretic, swathed my naked quarter-pounder body in Saran Wrap (long before Kathy Bates did so in *Fried Green Tomatoes*), and lowered myself into a bathtub of steaming hot water to sweat off another couple of pounds.

It worked. The next day when I hesitantly stepped on the scale at the enlistment station, I weighed one hundred and forty-*one* pounds. Hello, Uncle Sam!

4
UNCOOL

I am a nerd, bookworm, geek, whatever you want to call me.
I'm the type of person who would rather sit down
and read a good book than go out and party.
—Jacqueline Emerson

Reading in our backyard. Note the ugly cactus and stark Phoenix landscaping.

I've never been cool.

During high school, while the cool, popular girls were out on dates Saturday nights, I was either home watching *The Partridge Family* and Mary Tyler Moore, or devouring books like *Marjorie Morningstar,* Leon Uris's *QBVII,* and every Mary Stewart, Victoria Holt, and Phyllis Whitney mystery I could get my hands on.

A couple times a month I would go to the movies with a girlfriend to moon over Al Pacino in *The Godfather, Serpico, Scarecrow* ... Ryan O'Neal in *Love Story* and *What's Up Doc* ... or the sensitive Timothy Bottoms in *The Last Picture Show* and *The Paper Chase.* The seventies were a great decade for movies.

Some Saturdays, I would spend the night at my best friend Dawn's. In her bedroom, we took turns singing Donny Osmond's "Puppy Love" into our hairbrushes and belting out "Cabaret" a la Liza Minnelli. I loved Liza and wanted to *be* her.

My musical tastes were never in sync with the rest of my classmates.

While most of them were listening to Led Zeppelin, Black Sabbath, and Alice Cooper, I was listening to Sinatra, show tunes, and The Carpenters. One time, my creative writing teacher played some music in class on the bulky record player and told us to write what kind of response it evoked. He played hard rock—some band with a color in their name—and I wrote, *garbage cans smashing together.* Then he played an instrumental version of "Come Saturday Morning" that left the rest of the class groaning and writing, *cheesy elevator music,* while I dreamily imagined myself running in slow motion through a field of wildflowers to Bobby Sherman.

I was also busy reading the first issues of the new *Ms.* magazine, performing in the high school drill team, and becoming editor of the high school paper. I loudly proclaimed that women could do anything men could do, as proven by Billie

Jean King beating Bobby Riggs in the famous "Battle of the Sexes" tennis match in 1973.

To demonstrate my assertion, I challenged the guys, including my secret crush Rick Bartelt, captain of the basketball team, to a game of touch football with my girlfriend Sue and a few others. The guys kicked our butts, but only because I was unaccustomed to the feel of a football in my hands.

To nurse my feminist defeat, I secretly watched John Wayne in *The Quiet Man*. When The Duke grabbed Maureen O'Hara to him in a passionate lip-lock in his Irish cottage, my heart fluttered.

My senior year classmate Rick made my heart flutter too. I longed for the glorious Rick to notice me and ask me out, but the popular basketball player who reminded me of golden-boy Robert Redford in *The Way We Were* (only with brown hair) dated pom-pom girls and cheerleaders. I was the strident Barbra Streisand character, impassioned in my budding feminist cause, whom none of the boys wanted to date.

At the end of senior year, Rick wrote in my yearbook, "You're a good-looking girl, but you spend too much time being a man."

Jubilantly, I showed my best friend his words. "Look! He thinks I'm pretty!" The strains of "I Feel Pretty" from *West Side Story* played in my head.

The highlight of senior year was going to Las Vegas with my best friend and her parents after graduation and seeing LIZA in concert. Hearing my idol in person was a dream come true. I wanted to *be* her all over again and wondered how soon I could leave home to make my mark on Broadway and become best friends and roommates with Liza.

Sinatra wasn't playing the strip when we visited Vegas, but we did get to see Frank's good friends Steve Lawrence and Eydie Gormé—the older Sonny and Cher of the day. (Except Steve and Eydie could *both* sing.) As I listened to them croon the standards, I felt an almost spiritual connection to the music.

I've always been drawn to the spiritual. *Or was it more the idea of the spiritual?* After reading Leon Uris's *Exodus* about the founding of the State of Israel, and watching the subsequent movie with Paul Newman, I dreamed of going to Israel and serving on a kibbutz, where I would be nobly willing to die while fighting for my faith and my spiritual homeland.

Except I wasn't Jewish.

Then, after watching Ingrid Bergman lead more than a hundred Chinese children to safety in *The Inn of the Sixth Happiness,* I decided I wanted to become an overseas missionary instead. It appealed to my Protestant sense of goodness and purity.

But once I saw Debbie Reynolds singing and strumming her guitar in *The Singing Nun*, it was all over. I longed to become a nun—the ultimate example of purity and all that was good and noble—and join the convent.

In my high school Angel Drill Team uniform. (The marching came in handy in basic training.)

Except I wasn't Catholic.

I tried to join a convent once, but they wouldn't let me in.

After an angsty teenaged fight with my mom and new stepdad—a wrinkled atheist twenty years older than my mom who drove a Cadillac and owned a big house with a swimming pool—I ran away from home at sixteen, seeking solace with the sisters at a desert convent down the street. There I hoped to hide away from my family and the world. I would read, pray, and meditate in the wilderness sanctuary with the other sisters and till the soil for our daily bread.

The kind young sister in the pale blue habit who came to the gate encouraged me to go home and make peace with my folks. She said I was welcome to come back when I was of age, but meanwhile, where did I live?

Before she and the other approaching sister had a chance to call the cops—pre-cell phones, thankfully—I hightailed it down the dusty road to the nearest phone booth where I called a girl-friend who came and rescued me. Unfortunately, it was only for the night. When I returned home, I was grounded for a month.

So much for my good girl rep.

5

BOOT CAMP AND
UNSATISFACTORY EYEBROWS

That would be a good thing for them to cut on my tombstone:
Wherever she went, including here,
it was against her better judgment.
—Dorothy Parker

A week after the-thing-that-must-not-be-named, at nineteen, I said goodbye to my family and escaped Phoenix by joining the Air Force to see the world like my dreamer-dad.

San Antonio wasn't exactly what I'd had in mind.

Pulling KP duty, buffing dorm room floors, and field-stripping cigarette butts on base clean-up detail wasn't exactly the exciting military life I'd imagined after watching Lana Turner and other glamorous stars play World War II WACs in the movies—long before Goldie Hawn's turn in *Private Benjamin*.

"It is now 0500 hours. All airmen will be up, all airmen will be awake."

1975—the beginning of my Air Force career

Fifty pairs of bare feet, including mine, slapped the linoleum barracks floor. I grabbed my towel and raced ahead of the thundering herd, hoping to get in and out of the showers quickly before the rest of my female comrades-in-arms arrived. Ever since eighth-grade gym class when the rest of the girls already wearing bras teased my flat chest and white undershirt, I have never liked showering *en masse*.

After showering, pulling on our basic training uniforms, and making our beds, it was time for morning inspection. We stood at attention as our Gestapo-like sergeant training instructor (TI) began her rounds.

"Airman, do you call this a properly made bed?"

My eyes flicked to my regulation gray metal Air Force cot.

"Keep your eyes on me, airman!" the sergeant yelled two inches from my face.

"Ma'am, yes, ma'am."

"Is this a properly made bed?"

"Ma'am, no, ma'am."

"Well then I suggest you learn how to make it."

"Ma'am, yes, ma'am."

I quickly learned that the best way to make my bed as taut as the TI demanded was to lie down on the ugly linoleum, slide beneath my cot, and individually thread the tucked-in flat sheets and scratchy Army-green blanket through the chicken-wire bedsprings. One morning, as I was shoving the thick blanket through the small octagonal springs, tears rolled down the sides of my face and wet my hair.

"What am I doing?" I raged inwardly. "I'm a smart, inde-pendent, creative woman. Too smart for this Mickey-Mouse crap. How's this going to help me fulfill my dream of becoming a writer?" I flashed back to the conversation I'd had with the features editor of *The Arizona Republic* and *Phoenix Gazette* shortly before graduation. Marching my good-girl, award-winning high-school editor, seventeen-year-old self over to the city newspaper with a folder of my published news clippings, I announced I'd like a job as a reporter.

The editor flipped through my clips, skimming the stories. "You definitely have talent, but you're too young. We don't hire reporters without a college degree or at least some life experience."

Images of *His Girl Friday* and *Teacher's Pet* with Doris Day flashed in my head. "I thought I could start out as a copy girl or maybe a cub reporter."

"That's just in the movies. Those black-and-white days are

long gone. We do have a receptionist/clerk-typist position available."

Clerk typist? Not in this universe. "Thank you for your time."

"Come back when you've got that degree or some life experience."

I sneezed as a dust bunny wafted past my face beneath my barracks bed. I was getting some of that life experience now. My recruiter's words echoed in my head: "Remember, basic training is not the real Air Force. It's just a six-week exercise in teaching you to follow orders."

One of those orders involved guarding the latrine while the rest of my flight mates ran and jumped through various obstacles in the requisite "confidence course." Just released from the base hospital after a bad bout of flu, I was thankfully exempt from the strenuous physical course. Instead, while my fellow airmen—the recent designation applied to all enlistees, regardless of gender—climbed walls and swung across scuzzy pond water, I had to snap to attention and yell, "Halt! Who goes there? State your business," whenever anyone approached the facilities. Only after the airman responded with their name, rank, and type of business—Number One or Number Two—could I allow them inside.

During those six weeks of following orders, I learned to roll my pantyhose into a jelly roll measuring exactly three-fourths of an inch in diameter, fold my panties into equal thirds, and wash my GI body with shampoo (body wash hadn't been invented yet) to keep my bar of soap immaculate. One minuscule piece of lint could earn a demerit (called a 341) from our by-the-book training instructor. I had received a 341, along with everyone else in my dorm, during that first inspection.

"Airman, what do you call this?" the TI bellowed as she plucked my soap loose from its nesting place in its pink plastic flip-top case inside my locker.

"A bar of soap, ma'am?"

"Are you getting smart with me, airman?"

"Ma'am, no ma'am." I stood at attention at the foot of my cot, arms rigid at my sides, back ramrod straight, eyes fixed forward.

"Then I'll ask you again." She spit out the words in a staccato machine-gun clip. "Airman, what do you call this?" She brandished the bar of soap beneath my nose.

My eyes flicked over the brand-new Ivory I had just that morning unwrapped for my first shower at Lackland Air Force Base. After what felt like an interminable moment of intense scrutiny, I finally detected the offending protrusion beside her right index finger. "Ma'am, a soap bubble, ma'am?"

"Correct." She barked over her shoulder to her trusty two-striper assistant, "Airman Reed, issue this airman a 341 for having a dirty bar of soap in her locker."

"Yes, ma'am."

The TI sergeant moved on to the next quaking recruit while I accepted my first, but definitely not last, 341 of basic training.

"Airman, what do you call this?" she roared at the recruit one bed over.

That night, my fellow airmen and I wiped clean every single bar of Dove, Dial, and Ivory in our barracks and put them back in pristine condition into each locker drawer, not to see the light of day again until the six weeks of training were up.

My navy-blue fatigue pants were another problem.

"Airman, didn't your mama ever teach you to sew?" the TI boomed when she first caught sight of my two-inch, unevenly spaced, and crooked stitches meant to resemble a hem.

"Ma'am, no ma'am."

"That's the sorriest lookin' pair of pants I've ever seen." The sergeant turned to her assistant. "Airman Reed, have you ever seen such an ugly piece of sewing in your natural born days?"

"No ma'am, I don't believe I have."

Sewing has never been my strong suit.

Neither has physical fitness, which was another part of our daily regimen. As we ran laps around the track, our TI would shout encouragement. "Come on, ladies, get those lazy legs moving! And don't forget to hold your imaginations."

Uncle Sam did not want his male band of recruits, who marched past the track daily, to be distracted by our feminine charms, so every female airman had to run with her fists pressed beneath her bouncy GI breasts to hold them in place. We also had to endure beauty class in place of weapons training. When I joined the Air Force in early 1975, women weren't allowed in combat. Thus, it was unnecessary for female airmen to learn how to shoot a rifle unless they were going into the Security Police. Instead, while all the male airmen underwent their M-16 training, we got beauty tips.

"Remember, ladies," the beauty training sergeant instructed, "your hair cannot extend beneath your collar, and makeup should always be understated. No heavy eyeliner or bright red lips. We don't want you looking like ladies of the evening. Soft pink or peach lipstick is preferred. We don't want any bushy eyebrows either." She clapped her hands. "Split in half and form two lines. Ten-hut."

Our entire flight snapped to attention as the sergeant and her assistant made their way down each line, one airman at a time, plucking our unsatisfactory eyebrows.

Two things made basic training bearable: the candy bars we got to buy once a week at the BX (Base Exchange) and Sunday mornings. Everyone looked forward to chapel on Sunday, even the atheists. It was the only moment of beauty and respite during the week. Inside the off-white building, I would close my eyes, breathe in the scent of beeswax, and let the lovely old hymns carry me away—far away from the unrelenting discipline and constant, collective squelching of any spark of individuality or creativity. In church, no one could hear our TI scream. For an hour each week, chapel made me feel human again and free.

Our sergeants granted us some freedom during Holy Week too. Easter fell during the fourth week of training, and Uncle Sam wanted to acknowledge this most holy of days, so an unexpected treat was ordered: TV. Television was usually off-limits since they banned entertainment during basic.

When we first arrived at Lackland, any portable radios we had brought with us in those pre-iPod and iPad days were confiscated and locked away. There was a big console color TV in the barracks, never turned on. Every time we walked past the dayroom door, we shot longing looks at the beautiful boob tube sitting unplugged and unloved in the corner. Much to our delight, in the spirit of the Easter season, the powers-that-be allowed us to watch *The Ten Commandments* on Good Friday.

Charlton Heston had never looked so good.

Yul Brynner as Pharaoh's other son wasn't too shabby either, except for the goofy side ponytail he wore. The biblical epic, which includes the great Anne Baxter line, "Oh Moses, Moses, you splendid, stubborn adorable fool!" was also a good reminder that God would deliver us out of boot camp, just as he'd delivered the Israelites.

But the most spiritual moment during basic training came when Airman Reed, our assistant TI, stood at the end of our barracks bay and serenaded us to sleep one night with "The Lord's Prayer."

It was like all of our mothers collectively tucking us in.

6

JANE AUSTEN, GAS MASKS, AND
BARRY MANILOW

There is something so amiable in the prejudices of a young mind,
that one is sorry to see them give way
to the reception of more general opinions.
—Jane Austen

After basic training, I spent four weeks of tech school in Biloxi, Mississippi, the sweaty armpit of America. Then I received orders for Europe.

Europe. That ancient world of great art and literature that I had only read about in books and seen in movies. I couldn't wait to walk down those antique streets and drink in all the history and beauty for my dad and me. Dad had always dreamed of going to Europe but wound up doing his naval duty in Asia instead.

My first weekend in Germany, I walked off base to the nearest bus stop in the town of Bitburg near the Luxembourg border. Bravely, I boarded the bus, German currency in hand.

"Trier," I said.

"*Fear mark foomshish.*"

"English?"

The conductor shook his head. *"Nein. Fear mark foomshish."*

I shot a desperate look at the first few rows of passengers that included several women with hairy armpits. "Anyone speak English?"

They looked at me blankly and shook their heads.

There was a commotion from the back of the bus. A young boy walked shyly forward. "I speak ze English."

"Thank you so much." I held out my hands with the confusing German Deutsch marks and assorted coins.

He plucked four single bills from my hand and five coins with the number ten on them. *"Vier Mark, fünfzig."*

"Danke Schoën." I offered up a quick, internal thanks to Wayne Newton for the only German I knew.

Forty-five minutes later, I stepped off the bus into another world. I wandered in a daze through the market square in the oldest city in Germany, called the "Rome of the North," barely able to breathe. Beautiful baroque buildings in Easter-egg colors connected to creamy stone structures with intricate laceworks of timber on their fronts. I saw monument after monument, including a cathedral, basilica, and a pink palace. My first palace. All that was missing was a prince.

I passed by carts of fresh fruit, flowers, and souvenirs. Bratwurst stands wafting aromas of *pommes frites* and sizzling meat swelled my carnivore heart. That heart stopped when I reached the four-story Porta Nigra—the largest surviving Roman gate north of the Alps, built in AD 180.

Phoenix didn't have anything like that. Neither did Racine.

As I stared at Trier's ancient black gate from the Middle Ages, I wished my dad were there to share it with me. I recalled all those happy childhood hours of him wistfully telling us about the famous monuments of Europe and all its great art, hoping to see them in person someday.

The next afternoon, a rainy Sunday, I stretched out on my barracks bunk and picked up the parcel my mom had given me at the Phoenix airport before I left on my first overseas assignment. "This is your dad's novel he started years ago." She handed me a dog-eared manila envelope with my father's name scrawled on it. "I'd like you to finish it for him since you're going to be a writer someday."

My dad wrote? I never knew that. I never saw my father writing, only painting, always painting, whenever he could, or taking pictures with his Minolta after he started selling cameras at Turnstyle, the local department store. Dad was as good at photography as he was at painting. He took third prize in a national photo competition once and won a small wooden clock that I still have today. I fumbled for the oversized envelope in Mom's outstretched hands.

One week later, in Germany, I gingerly removed the thick manuscript typed on 1950s dime store wood-pulp paper and began reading the story of a young dreamer's search for truth and beauty beyond the confines of his small, conventional midwestern town. As I read, tears splashed onto the cheap tan pages. The story continued with the small-town dreamer sailing to Europe and exploring the wondrous places he had only visited in books. Paris. London. Trier.

Trier? I stopped reading mid-sentence. Dad had never been to Germany. How did he know about the small city of Trier? It's not like it was Berlin or Frankfurt.

It was a sign.

I clutched the manuscript to my then-perky breasts, scrunched my eyes shut, and raised my face heavenward. "Thank you," I breathed. That afternoon, I vowed to finish my dad's book for him someday. When I became a real writer.

That someday was still a far-off dream. Heeding the Phoenix editor's advice, I knew I needed life experience before attempting to write.

So, I set about getting that experience. During the midst of the sexual revolution, I shed my high-school wallflower skin and went on dates most Saturday nights. Heady stuff for the girl never asked to prom or homecoming. It was definitely raining men for women in the seventies at overseas bases. With more than a dozen men to every woman on base, we could have our pick of just about any man we wanted. Exciting times.

At Bitburg Air Base, Germany, with my cool 1970s tapestry dorm room decoration.

Once, in the dead of winter, just after midnight, I had a secret assignation with my paramour of the moment and had planned a surprise for him. I'd showered, shaved my legs, moisturized, put on my sexiest makeup, sprayed on some Jontue, and donned my outfit: black ankle-strapped stilettos. Nothing else. Covering my naked body with my mid-thigh-length coat edged with fake fur trim, I tiptoed down the empty hallway of the women's dorm. Unfortunately, when I turned into the stairwell, it wasn't empty. One of my fellow dorm mates sat on the top stair having an earnest break-up-sounding conversation with her boyfriend, who was sprawled across the bottom three steps, legs stretched out in front of him as he leaned his head to the side and looked up at her.

Great. Now what was I going to do? They had already seen me, and I'd noticed my date's car pulling up out front. I decided to go for it and hope her boyfriend wouldn't have a bird's eye view.

"Hi, guys," I said, clacking down the stairs in my stilettos.

Maybe he got a glimpse because he became my boyfriend a few weeks later. I'll never know if that was the moment, but I'll always suspect.

I never let any of my dates get too close. It helped that I was usually attracted to older, unavailable men. Looking for dad in all the wrong places.

One forty-year-old sergeant, two years younger than my father would now have been had he lived, introduced me to Rhine wine, poker, and the music of Barry White. "Can't Get Enough of Your Love Babe" became "our song." I felt safe and protected in his older arms—a safety I had not known since my dad died—and fell head over heels as we snuggled and talked about our happily ever after and the pretty café-au-lait babies we would have. Apparently, the sergeant *could* get enough of my love. He never left his wife as he'd promised.

Jerk.

Another GI once told me I was a dead ringer for Sheena Easton, his major pop-star crush and "the most beautiful woman ever." That line got him a night of passion. My dateless high school years had left me insecure about my attractiveness to men, and compliments like that proved my worth and made me feel pretty. The next night, I overheard the same GI tell a pretty blonde she was a dead ringer for Olivia Newton-John, his major pop-star crush and "the most beautiful woman ever."

Creep.

Then there was the man who vowed his eternal love and devotion and slept with my big-boobed girlfriend after insisting I was the only woman for him.

Bastard.

I met my share of bastards in the military. A few good men, too, but by that point, I did not trust any man, so the good ones fell by the wayside.

In 1975, when I first arrived on base in Germany at the tender age of nineteen, our three-story women's barracks housed about eighty female airmen. During my three-block walk to work that first day, clad in my dress blues and low quarters (ugly black leather oxfords), I passed several wolf-whistling GIs who asked me what floor I lived on. I later learned, courtesy of a couple good ol' boy sergeants, that the men had labeled each floor of the women's dorm: dykes, whores, and wannabe wives.

Way to make us feel all warm and welcome.

My first week on base I was surprised by how many men who I had never met knew my name. "Hi, Laura, lookin' good." "Laura, wanna go out with me?" "Hey, Laura, how 'bout you and I go to the submarine races?" One of the girls in the dorm explained that every time assignment orders arrived in the base personnel office announcing the impending arrival of another single female airman, the male clerks would spread the particulars among the other GIs about the "fresh meat" soon to appear.

That fresh meat label followed us around base.

Sometimes, when I didn't feel like eating breakfast in the chow hall, I would stop by the snack bar on the first floor of the building where I worked for an egg sandwich. One morning in particular stands out. When I arrived, wall-to-wall men in uniform packed the place. Not a woman in sight. There were no empty seats, and a cluster of male airmen stood at the counter placing their orders. I walked in and all heads swiveled my way. Was it just my imagination or were they licking their lips? Why did I suddenly feel like Little Red Riding Hood? Tempted to take my picnic basket and flee, I decided to stand my ground. After all, I was also a proud member of Uncle Sam's Air Force and had just as much right to eat there as the men did.

A couple older men jumped up to offer me a seat, but I politely declined with a smile so as not to give offense. God forbid I give offense to any man. (Thank you, 1960s good-girl upbringing.)

As I walked to the front at a normal pace so they wouldn't sense my fear, I could feel every eye on me stripping me naked. After what seemed like an eternity, I made it to the counter and placed my order to go. Every minute that passed made me feel more exposed and vulnerable. Behind me, the wolves began chomping their teeth.

At last, the short-order cook handed me my sandwich. Thanking him, I glanced up at the overhead clock.

"Whoa! Is that the time?" I said loudly. "Sergeant Black is gonna kill me for being late."

Having established a plausible excuse for my hasty exit—as well as the higher rank of the boss expecting me—I hurried out of the woods, a.k.a. scary sex slave dungeon, before the slathering pack could attack.

No more breakfast egg sandwiches for me.

After Germany, I received orders for my new assignment: England. Land of Shakespeare, Jane Austen, and warm beer.

I fell hard for Merrie Olde England. I fantasized about living in a thatched-roof cottage nestled in the rolling green hills of the English countryside when my enlistment ended and writing the Great American novel as I sipped a perfect cup of tea with milk and sugar. I would traipse through the Lake District picking daffodils while quoting Wordsworth and visit the Yorkshire moors looking for my Heathcliff. On the weekends, my well-bred English boyfriend, named Ian or Colin, would squire me to London where we would take in the latest plays in the West End and hobnob with the London literati.

Regrettably, the only Brit I ever dated was balding fifty-three-year-old Stanley, a blind date set up by a stranger on a train. (Okay, she was more like a casual acquaintance I'd briefly met through friends of friends, but "stranger on a train" sounds more mysterious and Hitchcockian.) I was riding the train from London to Oxford when this elegant, sophisticated woman a few years older than me, who resembled Ali MacGraw, only more enigmatic, pulled out a monogrammed gold compact and opened it to check her makeup.

"What a beautiful compact."

"Thank you." She smiled. "It was a gift from a friend."

"Boyfriend?"

"No, just one of my dates."

"I'm clearly dating the wrong men. I never get gifts like that."

"If you like, I could set you up with someone," she said in her posh, upper-crust English accent.

"Go for it," I said in my not-so-upper-crust midwestern accent.

"Do you mind if he's a bit older? I know a London gentleman who deals in antiques."

"I like older; bring on the antique," I said, with visions of Cary Grant filling my head.

A week later, I opened the door of my quaint English

cottage to Mel Brooks instead. In high heels, I was nearly a foot taller than my date. I told myself not to let Stanley's shortness bother me. I mean, look at Woody Allen and Diane Keaton. Al Pacino and Diane Keaton. Cuddly Dudley Moore and all his taller girlfriends.

As an older man, Stanley was bound to be wise and interesting, and, since he was English, refined and well-bred. Add in the London antiques dealer aspect, and I knew he would ooze culture and sophistication.

He oozed all right. During dinner at the lovely country inn, Stanley attempted to impress me with his knowledge of French by yelling to the waiter, "Gar-cone, Gar-cone!" After that, it was a rapid downhill slide into the roast beef and Yorkshire pudding.

Mel Brooks morphed into Benny Hill as my ribald raconteur entertained me with one dirty joke after another while I slunk lower in my seat. On the way home, I kept up a steady stream of patter about the land of the free and home of the brave to curtail Stanley's crude anecdotes. When we arrived at the stone cottage I shared with my Air Force roommate Diane, I was dismayed to discover Diane had gone out for the evening, leaving me alone with my lusty Lothario.

Inwardly, I began to hyperventilate. Outwardly, I kept my cool, knowing I couldn't let my date see my fear. The Yorkshire Ripper, the seventies version of Jack the Ripper, was roaming the countryside then, and I was afraid of being home alone with this blind date from hell that I didn't know from Adam. I tried to be polite and pleasant, yet not too pleasant. Stanley, who was a little drunk, moved in for the kill. He attempted to plant a wet, sloppy kiss on my lips, while at the same time trying to slip his hand down my dress.

I sidestepped his clumsy advances. Politely, of course. I didn't want to anger him. Then, with a flourish, Stanley pulled a gold bracelet out of his pocket and drunkenly dangled it before my face as he leered at me and made me an offer he thought I could not refuse.

Now I knew how my acquaintance on the train got her gold compact. Call me naïve.

When my drunken date repeated his offer a little more obnoxiously, I did what any self-respecting woman interested in saving her skin and virtue—even if it was a bit tarnished—would do. I lied. I told Stanley I needed to check in with the base because there were rumors we might go on alert (war games) that night.

"Excuse me while I just go check," I told him as I headed to the foyer where the bulky English phone resided. This was back in the dialing days, and British phones made a loud, distinctive sound when dialed, so if I did not call, he would know. I kept my finger pressed down on the receiver cradle buttons while I dialed. Then I proceeded to carry on an animated, one-way conversation with the pretend duty watch sergeant that I made sure my date could hear. After loudly replacing the receiver, I arranged a chagrined look on my face and returned to the waiting Stanley.

"Well, that's the life of a soldier," I said regretfully. "I'm afraid I'll have to cut our evening short. I'm sorry, but I'm ordered to report to base immediately in full alert gear." I started to shepherd Stanley to the front door.

His eyes gleamed and drunken drool pooled in the corners of his mouth. "Cor, I'd love to see you in uniform."

I'll bet you would, you dirty old man. Forced to play out my war games pretense, I bounded up the stairs, making sure to lock my bedroom door behind me, and changed into my green fatigues and war gear.

"Right then, I'm ready," I said in a muffled voice as I descended the stairs.

Stanley gave me a slow onceover, starting at the toes of my steel-tipped combat boots, lingering on my bulky fatigues and field jacket, and finally coming to rest on my gas-masked face and helmeted head. Then my not-so-gentleman caller insisted on following me out to my car.

I unlocked my car door and extended my hand. "Thank you for a lovely evening," I said from the safety of my tightly sealed, kiss-proof, and way-too-warm rubber gas mask.

Stanley shook my hand, saluted, and watched as I drove away. Keeping a surreptitious watch in my rearview mirror as he followed me down the road, I puffed out a breath of relief into my sweaty sealed gas mask when Stanley finally turned and headed in the direction of the train station. I continued down the road a way, turned off onto a quiet country lane, pulled to the side, shut off my engine, and waited in the dark for twenty minutes just to be safe. Then I stealthily made my way back home and crept inside, dripping with sweat in my claustrophobic combat regalia.

Moral of the story? Beware of strangers on the train.

Before a date while stationed at RAF Upper Heyford, England.

My spiritual life was nonexistent at the time.

God hadn't saved my father from dying, and he hadn't saved me from one heartbreak after another. Nor had he saved the victims of the Son of Sam serial killer, or the 500-plus people in the fatal crash of two 747s in the Canary Islands in 1977. So why should I believe in him or any kind of organized religion?

On Sunday mornings, to drown out the archaic hymns emanating from the 300-year-old Anglican church next door, I would blare Barry Manilow or Donna Summer from the pink stone cottage where my roommate Diane and I lived in a small village in Oxfordshire. I was single, now twenty-one, living in Europe, and had a string of men at my disposal like Scarlett O'Hara. And just like Scarlett, I wasn't interested in getting tied down with a "passel of brats," unlike a lot of my fellow female airmen who dreamed of marriage to Mr. Right. Preferably a flyboy Captain Right (years before *Top Gun*), two or three kids, and the whole white-picket-fence routine.

Not me. I was having way too much fun flying a typewriter through Europe in Uncle Sam's Air Force as a—wait for it —*clerk typist.*

By the time my tour of duty ended, I'd skied in the Alps (okay, snowplowed into cars in the parking lot, but let's not quibble. I was on skis in the frickin' Alps! Were you?), volks-marched in Germany, glided through the canals of Venice in a gondola, and tried not to gasp in good-girl midwestern shock when I saw the women in the windows in Amsterdam's red-light district.

I did gasp at Winged Victory in the Louvre, swim in the Mediterranean, watch Yul Brynner polka across a West End stage in *The King and I*, eat snails in Paris and frog legs in Luxembourg, and drink ouzo in Greece. That ouzo left me winding through tables in a Greek taverna (tavern with an "a") doing a Zorba-like snake dance with the waiters and other drunken patrons smashing plates and yelling "Opa!" Additionally, I had checked out the Crown Jewels in the Tower of London, read Jane Austen and Oscar Wilde beneath Oxford's dreaming spires, and visited the Little Mermaid in Copenhagen. All things my dad would have loved and probably included in his manuscript.

I had also wept at the ovens of Dachau.

As I made my way through the World War II concentration camp with a group of fellow GIs on our way to celebrate Oktoberfest in nearby Munich, the lively chatter of our band of brothers and sisters ceased. We continued the tour in silence past the barbed-wire fence line.

Past the wrought iron gate with the words *Arbeit Macht Frei*: Work will make you free.

Past the wooden bunk beds in rooms designed to sleep 200 but slept 1,000.

Past the showers.

Past the crematorium.

Into the museum that housed a cavalcade of black-and-white photos telling the story of the more than 32,000 who'd died at Dachau—and those were just the documented deaths. I saw photos of row after row of skeletal bodies. Skin stretched over jutting bones that I couldn't distinguish as male or female. Mounds of corpses piled high like heaps of trash at the dump. The stark white ribcage of a man with his mouth stretched wide in a long, silent scream of agony.

I couldn't look anymore.

Hurrying out of the museum, another photo caught my eye. A group of beaming men and children in dirty striped pajamas clustered at the barbed-wire camp fence, raising their caps in the air and cheering as the American GIs liberated Dachau.

I held my head high, snapped to attention, and saluted.

7

TATTOOS, CARPE DIEM, AND THAT
TOPLESS BEACH

I never travel without my diary.
One should always have something sensational to read on the train.
—Oscar Wilde

During my military years, I'd occasionally read something that awakened my dormant spiritual side, like Catherine Marshall's *Christy* or *Jonathan Livingston Seagull*. But then the feeling would pass, and I'd be on to my next exciting adventure. I briefly considered getting a tattoo of the bestselling seventies spiritual seagull on my hip, but the Englishman in the dingy tattoo parlor in Oxford said he would have to draw it freehand, so I passed.

Instead, I got a not-so-spiritual discreet tat of two cherries, one with a bite out of it.

When I received my TDY (temporary duty) orders for two weeks in Italy and the island of Sardinia with about fifty other GIs from our English base, I learned that there were several nude and topless beaches on the Mediterranean island. Another new and exciting adventure!

I am going to sunbathe on one of those beaches, I vowed. *When in Rome. . .*

Not sure if I'd have the nerve to go completely *au naturel*, I determined to go topless at the very least to demonstrate that I wasn't a puritanical American but a cosmopolitan woman of the world, like Marlene Dietrich or Catherine Deneuve. (My prissy good-girl self would never dream of going topless, and I was quite nervous about doing so. But this was a whole new, sophisticated world, and I was determined to expand my horizons, free myself from those stuffy small-town shackles and start living like Rosalind Russell in *Auntie Mame*, who said, "Life is a banquet and most poor suckers are starving to death.") It was a once-in-a-lifetime opportunity. *Carpe diem* and all that.

Besides, I would never see any of those people ever again.

My roommate and I were forced to stay at the luxury beach hotel where the officers were quartered since the Italian air base where our fellow enlisted airmen bunked did not have accommodations for women. Hardship duty, I know, but it comes with the territory of keeping America safe for democracy.

That first night, over drinks at the hotel bar, we overheard a couple officers with their tongues hanging out say there was a nude beach a few hundred feet to the right of the hotel and a topless one about half a mile down on the left.

I set my sights on the topless one farther away, figuring I would have a better chance of not running into any officers there. I would not be completely nude either, which was a relief. (As another plus, it would eliminate the sand-in-delicate-places issue.)

The next afternoon, I got off work early and hurried back to the hotel to change. Except, what do you wear to a topless beach? No way was I going to stride through the hotel lobby with my exposed twenty-one-year-old breasts standing at attention.

I pulled on shorts and a sleeveless cotton blouse over my modest two-piece, tucked in the blouse, and looked in the mirror. Too many clothes to shed once I got beachside. I wanted to blend in with the easygoing Europeans and act as if sunbathing sans tops was something I did regularly. I did not want to draw attention to myself as I blushed and fumbled with buttons and zippers. It needed to seem effortless.

I lost the shorts but left on the cotton blouse, unbuttoned, as a cover-up. Then I slung a towel over my shoulder, grabbed my Agatha Christie and beach tote, and made my laissez-faire way down to the white sand. The beach was crowded with bronzed and glistening bodies of every age, shape, and size, and no one paid any attention as I spread out my towel and dropped down on it ever so casually. I surveyed the scene to make sure there were no drooling flyboys in the vicinity.

Satisfied the Mediterranean coast was clear, I shucked my blouse and nonchalantly draped a second towel around my neck, the ends landing at my midriff as I unhooked and removed the top of my two-piece. (I never wore a bikini. Too revealing.) Then I slathered on a little Coppertone, picked up my paperback, stretched out on my back, and divested myself of the second towel.

Half an hour later, I awakened to a terrible sound.

"Look! It's Airman Jensen!"

My eyes flew open to reveal a quartet of my superior officers—including the base chaplain—ringed around the bottom of my towel gawking, cameras slung around their necks. I immediately flipped over on my stomach.

"Nice cherries. Is that a bite out of one?"

Before any of the officers could raise a telephoto lens, I jumped up and ran for cover in the emerald sea, staying in the water until the officers moved on.

Important topless bathing tip: do not shave your legs before plunging into the ocean.

At the age of twenty-three, my Air Force enlistment ended. Homesick after five years abroad, I returned stateside, joining my family in California where they had moved while I was overseas.

Going-away pub lunch (with my English roommate Liz) before shipping home.

I didn't stay long.

My dirty old man stepfather with the balding head and big nose sniffed out my new woman-of-the-world status and figured I was fair game, so hit on me. Mom had sent him over to my apartment to hook up my new TV and stereo system. "Why don't you come too?" I said when she phoned to tell me my stepdad was heading over. "Then we can visit."

Please come. Please come.

"Oh, I've got too much to do around here. Besides, this way you two can have some father-daughter time."

Except he was *not* my father. Not. Even. Close. He was an arrogant and condescending jerk who treated my younger brothers like crap, always criticizing them, calling them stupid, and telling them they would never amount to anything. They proved him right. Both my brothers wound up on drugs and in jail while I was overseas.

I did not like being alone with my stepfather. He creeped me out. But I couldn't tell my mom; it would hurt her feelings. Before the jerk arrived, I made sure to put on a bra, baggy T-shirt, and loose jeans.

"Thanks for doing this," I said, faking a smile when I opened the door to the dirtbag's knock. "I really appreciate it. I'm just going to work in the kitchen while you're hooking up the electronics since I still have a lot of unpacking to do." I kept up a steady stream of small talk as I unpacked and he connected the stereo. "So, did you and mom watch *Jeopardy* last night? Is that one guy still winning?"

"No, he choked on Final Jeopardy."

"Oh, that's too bad, but it gives someone else a chance." I placed water glasses in the cupboard. "I know Mom's really looking forward to your trip to Reno this weekend."

"Yes. She loves her slots." He hacked into his handkerchief. "Could I have a glass of water?"

"Sure. Sorry." I rinsed out a glass and filled it with cold tap water. "Here you go."

"Thanks." He took the glass, grazing his hand against mine (Eww!) and drank a few swallows.

I gave an involuntary shudder he couldn't see and headed back to the kitchen.

"Why don't you sit and talk to me a while?" he said. "We never get a chance to talk."

"We've been talking since you got here."

"It's difficult to carry on a conversation when you're banging dishes around."

"I'm way behind in my unpacking."

"You can take five minutes to talk," he said, in a wheedling tone.

"Okay, but just five minutes. I really have a lot to do." I perched on the edge of the couch as far away from the creep as possible.

He asked about my college plans and the GI Bill. Then he leered at me. "I dreamed about you last night."

I jumped up from the couch and returned to the kitchen. "I really need to finish unpacking."

"It was a sexy dream," he continued, staring at me as he ran his tongue over his pruney, ancient lips.

"Not the kind of dream a father should be having about his daughter."

"You're not my real daughter. Not by blood."

"Maybe, but I've always thought of you as a father," I said, lying through my teeth, which I had involuntarily begun grinding. I had never thought of that jerk as my father, but it was all I could think of to deflect his advances and get him out of my apartment.

Inwardly, I shook. Outwardly, I played it calm and cool. The phone rang and I grabbed it off the wall. "Hello?"

"Hi, honey. How's it going over there?"

"Good, Mom, except I have this terrible headache. I really need to take some Tylenol and lay down."

"Oh, I'm sorry. Dick can always finish up in the living room while you're taking a nap."

"No, better not. It's one of those headaches I get where the least bit of noise is excruciating. I just need total silence and darkness. We can do this another time."

"Okay, honey. Make sure you take Extra-Strength Tylenol, and I hope you feel better. Can you put Dick on? I need him to pick up some things from the store."

"Sure. Here he is."

I handed my stepfather the phone through the pass-through, making sure our hands did not touch, grateful for the extra-long phone cord. "Mom needs to talk to you."

"Hi, honey," said the dirty old man. "Okay, milk and bread. Anything else? How about your favorite, butter-pecan ice cream?" He licked his lips again and sent me a lusty look.

I wanted to hurl.

"Okay, see you soon."

"Wait, don't hang up. I forgot to ask Mom something."

He gave me a look but handed the phone back.

Back home after five years in Europe.

"Hi again. I just wanted to confirm when Lisa and Josh are coming over for dinner and what you wanted me to bring?" I walked to the front door and opened it wide as I continued the conversation with my mother. "Thanks, Dick, I really appreciate your help. Now what was that, Mom?"

The dirty old man grabbed his toolbox and left. I bolted the door behind him and slid to the floor, shaking.

That night I had a nightmare. The same recurring nightmare I first had while stationed in Germany. The Nazis were chasing me, and no one would help me or hide me. I was running up stairs and down corridors, pounding on locked doors, seeking refuge and a hiding place but never finding one. I heard the pounding of the Nazi storm troopers' heavy boots drawing closer, ever closer, as I continued my frenzied ascent up more stairways, higher and higher until I reached the roof. I raced across the top of the roof as the Nazis thundered up the stairs behind me with their boots and guns. There was nowhere to hide, nowhere to go.

As they burst through the doorway onto the rooftop, I took a flying leap off the edge of the roof to the building next door, landing like *To Catch a Thief's* cat burglar John Robie (Cary Grant) on all fours. Still the Nazis kept on coming, relentlessly chasing me. I kept on running, desperately seeking sanctuary, a place to hide, and finding nothing but another roof edge. This time when I leapt across to the next building, I missed. Arms flailing, I began falling...falling...falling...

8

STEP-BALL-CHANGE, GRANOLA, AND DO-OVERS

Life isn't choreographed. That's why I fall down a lot.
—Sacha Duncan

After the wicked stepfather incident, I fled California, knowing that it would crush my mother if she ever found out that her second husband, who gave her every material comfort that my dad had never been able to afford, had hit on me.

Instead, I ran away. Far, far away.

Eventually, at twenty-five, I ended up in Cleveland, where I discovered a group of like-minded artsy friends when cast in the chorus of a community theater production of *Guys and Dolls*.

I played a good-time-girl with smoky eyes and pouty Brigitte Bardot lips, courtesy of my friend Curt's stellar makeup skills.

Soon I was sharing a brownstone with three other artists, all actors, singers, and dancers, who performed regularly in town.

9

In full makeup for Guys and Dolls.

I had done a little acting overseas, playing one-half of a squabbling couple in a British comedy and getting the lead in the English pantomime (panto) of *Aladdin.* In English panto, the *principal boy* is always played by a woman in tights and the panto *Dame* is played by a man in drag. I played the principal boy (the only time I will ever appear onstage in tights). Double entendres fly and sight gags abound, like our genie not-so-accidentally popping the Dame's balloon boobs with his wand. Yes, wand. Our genie was gender-confused.

As Aladdin, one of my lines was "Uncle, where's the lamp?" Only thanks to my nasal Racine accent, it came out "la-a-a-a-mp" and the proper British audience who pronounce it "lahmp" erupted in laughter.

You can take the girl out of Wisconsin but not Wisconsin out of the girl.

In Cleveland, when we all auditioned for *West Side Story,* I was the only artsy roommate not cast. I gave a great reading as the gum-smacking girlfriend of one of the Jets but stumbled over my two left feet during the group-dance-number audition. I never could step-ball-change. Some of us can dance, others just watch Fred and Ginger.

One of my roommates, who had not come out of the closet yet, was a great dresser with a fabulous sense of style. Since I was usually indifferent to clothes in general and did not care about the latest fashion, John made it his mission in life to take me under his sartorial wing and give me a head-to-toe makeover. Soon I was twirling around the apartment humming "I Feel Pretty."

John and I became best friends and went everywhere together: restaurants, musical theater shows, clubs, and old movies. After watching Hitchcock's *Vertigo*, John told me I looked like Kim Novak when she was brunette, thus sealing our friendship for life. My new best friend was artistic, fun, safe, and so different from the military men I had known. He was also drop-dead gorgeous.

Naturally, I developed a crush. I always was attracted to unavailable men. Not that there's some deep, psychological reason for that or anything.

That crush deepened on the gala opening night premiere of the fresh-from-Broadway play *Nicholas Nickleby*, when unbeknownst to me, John ran down the backstairs in his tux, hurried around our brownstone, raced up the front steps, and rang the doorbell. When I opened the door—wearing the gorgeous navy, off-the-shoulder dress John had picked out— there stood my handsome date, smiling, with a corsage in his hand. I had told John about my dateless high school years and how I never went to prom, but that it wasn't a big deal.

He knew differently.

Occasionally we would go to a movie *en masse* with the rest of our roommates and assorted hangers-on of the moment. One such outing was to the just-released *Chariots of Fire* with the soaring Vangelis music and men running down the beach in their underwear. I munched on hot buttered popcorn and lusted over my beloved England on-screen. When the devout Scottish runner, and soon-to-be missionary, Eric Liddell said in his thick Scottish brogue, "God made me for a purpose, but he also made me fast. And when I run, I feel his pleasure," my soul clenched.

His words rekindled my dormant spiritual yearning. I wanted a relationship like that. To know that I had a purpose in life, and to feel God's presence and his pleasure. I tried to discuss this spiritual yearning with my best friend, but he was a lapsed Catholic and closeted so did not have the greatest opinion about the church in general. Consequently, I didn't do anything spiritual other than watch Franco Zeffirelli's *Brother Sun, Sister Moon* and fall for Saint Francis of Assisi.

I flitted from one thing to the next, making bad decisions and searching for something, or someone, to fill the emptiness.

I took a couple classes at a community college in Cleveland and fell in love with English literature and writing all over again. I tried to share that love with John, but he got bored and wanted to talk about the latest fashion and theater gossip or go dancing at the clubs. I was bored with the clubs and wanted something more. Something substantial. Something real. Something I had been longing for my whole life.

Returning to the Golden State at twenty-seven, I enrolled in Humboldt State University in Northern California's coastal redwoods—three-hundred miles north and several hours away from my creepy stepfather. Humboldt sits on a high hill at the edge of a coastal redwood forest with drop-dead views of the Pacific Ocean. God's country. Redwoods everywhere. Tallest trees in the world. Their perfume blankets the college and makes it smell like a Christmas tree lot all year long.

I didn't have enough money for a car, so I rented a room in the granola town of Arcata, which houses the college. I walked everywhere and made some new friends. Lottie, a belly dancer and one of my hippie, feminist friends, invited me to a potluck, an outdoor gathering of women. When I arrived in my white cotton sundress and cute sandals bearing a tuna casserole with crushed Lay's potato chips on top, I saw more breasts of every shape and size than I had seen on the topless beach in Sardinia.

I longed for a hairy male chest.

Finally, I spotted one hairy chest in the sea of breasts, but it was not male. I set down my Pyrex tuna casserole amidst a bounty of sprouts, beans, and veggies in colorful crockery, grateful I had not brought the pot roast I had initially considered.

At Humboldt, I majored in English and belatedly began to pursue my lifelong dream of becoming a writer. I began reading Sylvia Plath; studying the poetry of Byron, Shelley, Keats, and Wordsworth; and writing essays. Early in my first semester, one of my English professors asked me to stay after class. All my neurotic insecurities bubbled to the surface. *Was my latest essay that bad?*

"Are you an upper division student?" the professor asked.

"No. A freshman."

"And what's your major?"

"English."

"What do you plan to do after you graduate?"

"I, uh, hope to become a writer someday."

"You already are," he said, handing me my essay with a red A-plus at the top.

"I am?"

"Yes. Your writing is some of the best writing I've seen cross my desk in a while. It's rich, fluent, and natural."

"It is? *Really?*"

With the *Chariots of Fire* theme song filling my head, I floated home in a slow-motion haze of ecstasy, replaying the professor's words of praise over and over again, knowing at last I had found my purpose and was on my way to the life I'd always dreamed. I had been searching for this exact moment for more than a decade, ever since my dad died. In all the places in Europe, in all my adventures and life experiences, in my artsy Cleveland days, in each relationship, and every time I started college anew. I'd finally found what I'd been looking for.

Three years before U2 began searching.

Back at the apartment I shared with a woman who worked at the university, I discovered the GI Bill check I had been waiting for still had not come. The check I needed to pay for school, rent, and groceries. Thank you, governmental red tape.

A month later, the check still had not arrived. By now, I was flat broke and couldn't find a job. Not in that economically depressed area, the poorest county in California. Not even a house cleaner or waiter job. One guy offered me a position as a manicurist, but I told him I bite my nails. Different kind of manicurist—he meant harvesting marijuana from a local pot field.

My just-say-no-to-drugs good-girl recoiled in white-bread horror. "But that's illegal!"

I didn't get the job.

I didn't get my GI Bill check either. Jobless, hungry, out of groceries, and down to my last quarter. By this point I didn't have even one dollar to my name. No way was I going to ask my parents for help and be beholden to my creepy stepfather. My roommate had already paid my share of the rent for the past two months. I couldn't keep relying on her. What's a girl to do?

The Nazi nightmare returned in force.

"Help," I prayed.

God answered my prayer. At least I thought so at the time. Out of nowhere, some former coworkers called with a job offer across the country. It seemed too good to be true, but I couldn't see any other alternative. So, I packed up all my possessions and took the job, even though it meant moving out of state and quitting school. The school by the beach and the gorgeous redwoods. The school with the English classes I loved. The school where I got an A-plus on my essay and the professor told me I was a writer.

But when you have no other options, you do what you must. I could always return to school later, right? People did it all the time. No biggie. Now was the time to suck it up, be a grown-up, and start earning my way again. In this resilient, grown-up state of mind, I left behind everything for this heaven-sent job opportunity back East.

Only it was not heaven sent. There were fringe benefits, but my new employer wanted them from me.

I fled back to California, courtesy of my long-delayed GI Bill check—just enough for airfare and two suitcases—forwarded from my roommate. I had to leave the rest of my possessions behind, including antiques from my beloved England. Now I really had nothing. No job. No stuff. No school. No money. No life.

A heavy weight descended upon me. There was no point in going on. I was twenty-seven years old and felt seventy-seven. A used-up piece of trash in the casual-sex gutter left over from the anything-goes seventies.

Beneath my I-am-woman-hear-me-roar feminist exterior, that took an active part in the feminist and sexual revolution of the day, lurked an old-fashioned romantic raised on fairy tales, John Wayne, and Doris Day, the perennial virgin. At heart, I was the puritan good-girl Doris longing for the swoony Rock Hudson or macho John Wayne to come along and sweep me off my feet.

No man was going to ride in on a white horse and sweep *me* off my feet. The only place they would sweep me was down the gutter drain. I was so weary of it all. I just wanted to go to sleep and not wake up. If I had had a gun, I would have.

Despondent at the failure of my life, and seeing no reason to go on, I huddled on the floor of my empty rented room with its single bed, trying to decide the best way to end it all. Should I slash my wrists, the preferred suicide of choice in many of the books I had read and movies I had watched, even though the sight of blood makes me squeamish?

Standing outside my body, detached from the scene as if it were happening to someone else, I watched myself push up off the floor like a sluggish automaton and shuffle down the hall in a daze to the bathroom. There I listlessly retrieved my pink plastic disposable razor and held it up before me. Sitting atop the closed toilet seat, I squinted at the razor, trying to figure out how to remove the blade. Finally, realizing it was impossible, I gave up and started sawing away.

Grasping the pink plastic stem in my right hand, I pressed the head of the razor against the pale tender skin on the inside of my left wrist and drew the blade across in a slow, horizontal motion. Faint pinpricks of red formed on the pastel skin surface with its diagonal blue veins crisscrossing beneath the base of my hand. I drew the pink razor across again in the other direction, then back again, resulting in a few more infinitesimal red pinpricks. I tried the other arm, shifting the razor to my nondominant left hand and awkwardly trying to saw at the tender skin of my right wrist, but the blade was dull, and it didn't work. It hurt. (Years later, I learned if you really want to slash your wrists effectively, you should do it in a vertical motion and use a proper single-edge razor blade.) I dropped the pink razor in the trash and opened the medicine cabinet, searching for another exit.

Maybe an overdose of sleeping pills as the movies always showed?

I rummaged through the sparse cabinet I shared with my

older roommate, but there were no sleeping pills. Just Ex-Lax, which wouldn't create the desired effect. Too messy for this prissy girl who likes things neat and tidy.

Spotting a bottle of aspirin, I opened it and tipped the contents into my hand. Five pills landed in my palm. Holding my nose, I popped all five aspirin in my mouth at once, took a drink of water, and gagged. I have always had a problem swallowing pills. Why should it be any different now? Some of the pills didn't go down properly, and the remaining aspirin on my tongue began to dissolve, leaving a bitter taste. *Blech.* Gagging again, I spit out the chalky substance and scooped up mouthfuls of water to rid myself of the terrible taste. Still, it remained. I scrubbed my tongue furiously with Crest.

Returning to my denuded bedroom, minus my favorite *Gone with the Wind* and art posters from my time in Europe, I sank to the floor where I contemplated carbon monoxide poisoning like Audrey Hepburn in *Sabrina* until Humphrey Bogart intervened. Except I didn't have a car or even a garage.

That left drowning, but I've never been a water baby, and I'm afraid of heights, so jumping off a bridge wouldn't work either.

What a loser. I couldn't even succeed at suicide.

Dully, I curled up in a fetal position on the carpet and fell asleep. An hour or two later, the shrill ringing of the telephone woke me up. My mother's familiar voice came over the line. Her mom-radar had gone off down in Sacramento, and she knew something was wrong. Hearing the desolation in my voice confirmed it. Mom jumped on her parental white horse and galloped up to Humboldt to bring me home.

Having no other options, I moved back in with my parents temporarily, making sure to never be home alone with my stepfather. Under my mother's loving ministrations, the despair receded. In short order I got a secretarial job, a car, and a new professional wardrobe. Things started looking up.

On the surface.

Underneath, where the-thing-that-must-not-be-named slumbered, nothing had changed. I was still a worthless piece of trash in the gutter. The hopelessness and feelings of desolation returned.

A month after my return home, I found myself on the doorstep of some old Air Force friends I had known while stationed in England. Over the years, Matt and his wife Ann had become surrogate parents of a sort to me until they went and became born-again Christians and got weird, even disposing of the cool in-house bar they used to have. I had not seen them in several months because their constant God talk turned me off. That night, however, I needed a friendly face.

Listlessly, I filled Ann in on my latest screw-up. "There's no reason to go on," I said. "What's the point? Life sucks. Men are pigs. There's nothing good—nothing that brings me joy. Not even *The Sound of Music*." One of my favorite things.

"You need Jesus."

This time when Ann talked about Jesus, I listened. I had tried everything else. I was no Bible-camp-counselor-Debbie glowing with goodness. I had broken most of the Ten Commandments and was basically the worst sinner I knew. How could God forgive me for my Technicolor past?

Ann prayed the obligatory "sinner's prayer" with me and had me repeat the words, which I did, awkwardly. Afterwards, she smiled at me through her tears and said I was now a brand-new creation; all my sins were washed away.

"Even the sex ones?"

"Yes. Your purity has been restored," she said, beaming. "You're now a virgin in Christ."

I didn't know virginity could be retroactive, but I was grateful for the do-over. I was a good girl once again. Just like Doris.

BURNING BOOKS AND ALMOST
HAPPILY EVER AFTER

*I think God made a woman to be strong and not to be trampled under
the feet of men. I've always felt this way because my mother was a
very strong woman without a husband.*
—Little Richard

"Feminists are feminists because of men. Because some man has hurt them," preached the soft-spoken pastor at Ann and Matt's small church, which I attended the first Sunday after my conversion.

I sat up straight in my metal folding chair in the preschool where the nondenominational church held its services on Sunday. *How did he know that? Did he have a secret window into my life?* Then he said something about husbands loving their wives like how Christ loved the church and gave himself up for her. He talked about the sacrificial way husbands are supposed to love and treat their wives. My eyes slid to his denim-jumpered, pretty wife whose adoring gaze confirmed the soft-spoken pastor practiced what he preached.

I wanted what *they* had. Deep down, I realized I had wanted it for many years. But I had not admitted it to myself, nor had I seen many first-hand examples of that kind of generous, unconditional love, other than my friends Ann and Matt and now this pastor and his wife. Must be a Christian thing.

That same night I went home and prayed for a husband.

The gentle, hippie-ish pastor and his sweet wife with gorgeous honey-blonde hair down to her waist—which would have blown all the Breck girls' hair out of the water—radiated love and joy to everyone. They were kind and welcoming and enfolded me into the bosom of their church. I began attending a weekly Bible study and started to learn more about the whole new world I'd joined.

Then I met a man. It's always a man.

This man I met at church. I saw him talking to the pastor after the service the second week and pointing to something in his Bible. A fat Bible that was heavily underlined and yellow-highlighted.

He looked up from his Bible and our eyes met. "Hi," he said.

"Hi," I said, looking down demurely and sliding a sneak peek at his left hand.

Matt introduced us. "Laura, this is Paul. Paul, Laura." My surrogate father proudly hugged my shoulder. "Laura just accepted the Lord two weeks ago."

"Welcome," Paul of the no-wedding-band-left-hand said with a smile.

A few nights later, I attended a game night for the church singles and young marrieds. During charades—my best game, next to Silver Screen Trivial Pursuit—I could feel Paul's eyes on me. After I was the first one to guess three movies in a row (jumping up, pumping my fist, and shouting, "Yes!"), he gave me an admiring look.

We began dating that weekend.

Paul was not married or gay. *Hallelujah!* He carried his Bible everywhere and could quote Scripture better than anyone. Paul wanted to become a missionary and convert heathens in third-world countries, which I learned was the most respected job in Christendom. I felt quite smug dating such a spiritual man. It didn't hurt that he was cute and had a beard. I have always had a thing for beards. (Think Javier Bardem, not *Duck Dynasty*.)

Happy at last to be dating someone available, wanting desperately to be loved, and still not knowing too much about this entire born-again Christian thing, I blindly went along with whatever my devout new boyfriend said.

"Stop dressing like a man."

I was belatedly doing the quirky Annie Hall thing with men's tweed jackets from the thrift store: funky ties, jeans, and boots. Paul said that our pastor's wife, with her floral, lace-trimmed dresses, was someone I should emulate. Thus, for him and my new conservative Christian world, I traded in my Annie Hall thrift-store look for demure, calf-length dresses and denim jumpers.

"Grow out your hair. A woman's crowning glory is her hair."

Goodbye cute Liza Minnelli pixie cut, hello lush Jane Seymour tresses.

"You spent more than $100 on that dress? The only dress that should cost that much is your wedding dress."

He said the "W" word! He's thinking marriage! I promptly sold my teal silk dress with Linda Evans *Dynasty* shoulder pads from Casual Corner (which had necessitated a month's worth of bag lunches) for five bucks at a garage sale.

My new Christian boyfriend did not like my library either.

"You have too many feminist books," Paul said. "They're getting in the way of your spiritual walk. That's why you're having a hard time with submission. Those books go against God's natural order. You're opening yourself up to demonic influence by having them around."

Really? I've never heard that before. Seriously? Does it say that in the Bible? O-kaaay, I'll donate them to Goodwill.

"No, then others will be corrupted by them," Paul said. "The only way to get rid of their evil influence and cleanse yourself from their impact is to burn them."

Burn *books*? That's what Hitler did.

"I want to write books someday," I said. "How can I burn them?"

Paul quoted Scripture to me about purging evil and said I must burn the books to be set free and to walk in the light.

I wanted to walk in the light and be a full-fledged, card-carrying member of the good-girl Christian club, never to return to the darkness and despair that had left me all alone and on the brink of suicide. Reluctantly, I finally agreed, and Paul built a fire in the fireplace.

But I couldn't do it. "Why don't *you* burn them?" I asked.

"No, you have to. It's the only way you'll truly be set free from your past."

Under my new boyfriend's watchful eye, I fed the sinful feminist books to the fire one by one—*Fear of Flying, The Female Eunuch, The Women's Room*, and more.

I wanted to throw up, until I saw Paul's face glowing love down at me. He pulled me up from the stool where I had been sitting, took me in his arms, and kissed me as the books blazed behind us.

Love and fear make you do stupid things. It was worth it because Paul *had* been thinking marriage. Less than a month later, he proposed. God answered my husband prayer! Finally, at twenty-eight years old, I was on the path to happily ever after.

My good Christian fiancé also hated homosexuality, which he called an *abomination*. "I'd rather have a rapist in my house than a faggot any day," Paul proclaimed one night when we were having dinner with his roommate Daniel.

My head swiveled from Paul to Daniel. How could the man I love say such an awful, hateful thing? Especially since I had recently shared with him the deep dark secret of the-thing-that-must-not-be-named. A secret I had told so few people I could count them on one hand.

When in a shaky voice I reminded my fiancé of that trauma, he was silent. His roommate, on the other hand, a sweet, kind friend from church, looked at me with eyes full of compassion and said, "I'm so sorry."

Tears leaked from my eyes and an involuntary shudder shook my body as I flashed back to that awful night in the fraternity room from nearly a decade ago. Instantly, I shoved those dark memories back down.

"Were you a virgin?" kind Daniel asked.

"No." Feelings of shame, followed by feelings of anger.

No, I wasn't the pure Doris Day who had saved myself for marriage—the Number One commandment for all single Christian women. But I thought that becoming born again had washed away my sex sins and restored the all-important virginity, but whatever. *And my not being a virgin makes it any less awful, why?* Because raping a chaste, untouched *good girl* would be an act of defilement. Taking away her purity. For a woman who has already given it up to some guy, it's not a big deal—she's already damaged goods. After all, I'm the one who went to a bar and got drunk and left with a guy I didn't know. Talk about asking for it.

At the time of my assault in 1975, I bought into that whole rape-culture mindset. I had already experimented with sex with a couple men in those "I am woman, hear me roar" days, so this was just adding more to the list. No biggie. Except I never intended to add so many at once.

Reminds me of the time in high school when I overheard some football jocks clustered around their lockers talking about "pulling a train" on a female classmate who had a reputation for being "easy." It disgusted me and all my good-girl friends. That nasty, dirty girl could forget about getting married. Who would ever want her?

After the-thing-that-must-not-be-named train ran over me, I felt damaged. Spoiled. *Who would ever want me or want to marry me?* That is why I held on so desperately to my fiancé, even after he said those awful words: "I'd rather have a rapist in my house than a faggot any day."

I did educate him. "A gay man is not going to go after a straight man," I said, thinking back to all my gay musical theater friends in Cleveland. My fiancé had clearly heard too many men-in-prison stories.

That night I had the scary-Nazis-chasing-me nightmare again.

I broke up with Paul right after that.

At least, that is what I wish I had done, what I *should* have done. But my need to be loved by a "good" man was so great, I overlooked all manner of sins on his part and hung in there. Paul wound up eventually dumping me instead. Naturally. Story of my life.

I wasn't good enough.

Smart enough.

Thin enough.

Christian enough.

And most importantly, pure enough.

I was soiled. Dirty. Like that easy girl in high school. Who would ever want to love, let alone marry, me? That is why my born-again virginity meant so much to me.

Apparently, it was not enough for my fiancé. A month or so after that painful dinner discussion with his roommate, Paul informed me he didn't "feel a peace" about marrying me. He had been on the fence about it for weeks, he said, and praying about it. Something he had not shared with me.

"It's just cold feet," everyone at church reassured me, "happens to most men."

"My feet are warm enough for both of us," I told Paul, steadfast and unwavering in my love and commitment to him. I knew we were meant to be together. After all, wasn't he the answer to my prayer?

Yet Paul's feet continued to grow colder. Until at last, one week before the wedding, as my new, pure-as-the-driven-snow white wedding dress hung expectantly on the back of my bedroom door, he called it off.

I was shattered. After all the jerks and creeps and my confusing bad-girl sexcapades, at last I had found a good man. A Christian man. A decent man. I should have known better. Not gonna happen. Not with my past. I felt unloved and unworthy and that no man would ever love me.

My "crowning glory" of long hair.

God loved me, though. That I knew in the deepest part of my

broken heart. I had just forgotten it for a while in the heady rush of my relationship with Paul. God would never leave me, no matter what. The Bible told me so. I clung to that. One of my church friends shared a Scripture that broke through my pain, Jeremiah 29:11: *"For I know the plans I have for you," declares the Lord, "plans to prosper you and not to harm you, plans to give you hope and a future."*

My future was no longer at that small church. I had to leave because it was too associated with my ex. Everyone there knew Paul had dumped me and felt sorry for me. They kept paint-bombing me with Bible verses or saying encouraging things like:

"God has a better plan."

"Everything happens for a reason."

"God's really got something special for you."

10

RAINING MEN AT THE MEGACHURCH

. . . and heaven have mercy on us all—Presbyterians and Pagans alike
—for we are all dreadfully cracked about the head
and desperately in need of mending.
—Herman Melville

That something special, I decided, was becoming a missionary to Africa. At least that was what I *thought* I was supposed to do. During my heartache after being dumped by the man I thought was the answer to my prayers, I immersed myself in the New Testament and soaked in all the red-letter words.

Like, *Love one another. Do not let your heart be troubled. Take courage. I am here. If any of you wants to be my follower, you must turn from your selfish ways, take up your cross and follow me.*

At night as I wept over the loss of a man who loved and left me, it brought back the pain and much greater loss of my dad who loved and left me when he died. I wept anew for my beloved father, and God the Father comforted me. The Psalms became my lifeline.

Grateful, I wanted to give up everything to follow Jesus and serve God as a missionary. Like Eric Liddell (*Chariots of Fire*), Gladys Aylward (the Ingrid Bergman missionary in *The Inn of the Sixth Happiness*), or my father's personal hero Albert Schweitzer, the Nobel prizewinner who gave up a brilliant concert career to open a hospital in Africa. I decided to go suffer for Jesus in Africa like Audrey Hepburn in *The Nun's Story*. Audrey wore a wimple better than anyone.

They wouldn't have me.

At thirty-one, I attended a major missions conference in the Midwest, full of zeal and missionary fervor, and began approaching the missions' organizations one by one to offer myself up for service to Africa. Digging ditches, building orphanages, whatever they needed. They turned me down. I did not have the right credentials. Who knew you needed a college degree to be a missionary? I felt dumped all over again. Until I met a Nigerian pastor in colorful robes, who gently explained that many of the people I planned to serve in his homeland were better educated than me. What exactly did I have to offer other than being the Great White Hope?

Oh.

Returning home, I went back to college, where I became editor of the school paper and started winning awards for my writing. Meanwhile, I had begun attending an evangelical megachurch where nobody knew me, or my failed relationship. I walked into the Friday night singles group and my hormones went into overdrive.

So. Many. Men. Single men. Of every shape and size, who all carried Bibles, prayed earnestly, and went to church every Sunday. It was a sign.

A couple women and a hot guy came over to welcome me. Definitely a sign. I found a seat as a cute guy with a mustache began strumming his guitar up front. He led the group of nearly a hundred in singing songs proclaiming God was an awesome God and the battle belonged to the Lord. I watched as many in the room closed their eyes, lifted their hands, and swayed to the music. The only thing missing was lighters.

"Okay, folks, time for prayer," the worship leader said. "Break up into small groups of four or five."

I exchanged a nervous look with the woman next to me. I wasn't sure how to pray aloud in front of people. What if I did it wrong? The only prayers I knew were the "Now I lay me" death prayer from childhood and the classic "Our Father, who art in heaven..." My seatmate led me to a couple other women, and we joined their group. I wiped my sweaty palms on my jeans before taking their hands and bowing my head.

One of the women began to pray. "Father God, we come before you, Father, and just ask, Father, that we open our hearts to you. Help us, Father, to receive the message you have for us tonight. Amen."

Over the next few weeks during prayer time, I discovered God had many names—Lord, Yahweh, Father, Abba, Jesus—and that "just" was an essential prayer word. "Lord, just bless us and be with us tonight. Help us to be mindful of you in all that we say and do. We just pray, Lord, that you would just help us to be a light in the world and to just praise you, Lord. Amen."

I had been taught prayer was a conversation with the Almighty, but this didn't sound like any conversation I had ever heard. "Hi, Bob, I just want to talk to you, Bob, and ask, Bob, if you could just help me, Bob, because, Bob, I want to make sure you know that I know your name, Bob."

Sometimes people prayed in tongues, which freaked me out. They spoke quite fast in a foreign language not available on Berlitz tapes. I'd learned about tongues being a "gift of the spirit" at the first small church I attended. But that soft-spoken, Jesus-like pastor taught that tongues was another form of praise, and if someone spoke in tongues during the service, there would always be an interpretation because God was a God of order, not confusion. One guy at that first church who prayed in tongues was always mad and yelling he didn't buy the right car.

"IshouldaboughtaHonda, I shouldaboughtaHonda." (An editor friend mentioned a famous comedian might have said the Honda line, so I looked it up and found a YouTube clip from 2014 with a young comedian I had never heard of saying it. Since my friends and I were saying it in the '80s long before YouTube, when that comedian was around eleven, I'm claiming it on behalf of '80s evangelicals everywhere.)

One night during prayer time, the singles pastor asked if anyone wanted to pray "to receive the gift of the Holy Spirit." Not exactly sure what that meant, but eager to receive whatever God wanted to give me, I raised my hand along with several others. The pastor and a couple members of the leadership team led us into a smaller room, where we all sat cross-legged on the floor in a circle with our heads bowed as he prayed for us to be filled with the Holy Spirit.

Soon people on both sides of me began speaking in tongues. It reminded me of the guy from my last church except this sounded more like IshouldaboughtaHyundai. (I think that was around the time the economy started to go south.) Shortly, everyone around me was speaking in tongues, and I had nada. I was praying in earnest, wanting to be filled with as much of God's Spirit as possible, to be as close to him as I could. I did not get the gift of tongues, but I did feel suffused with warmth and God's love.

And that was good enough for me.

I loved that church. I liked the sermons. I liked the hip, contemporary Christian music. And I especially liked the fact that it was not just married people with young families. There I did not feel like the lone ranger, as I had at the smaller church. I also liked the emphasis on individuality and creativity. My first Sunday at the megachurch I saw a lot of teens, twentysomethings, and thirtysomethings in shorts and flip-flops, jeans and T-shirts, or leather. There was also multicolored hair, men with ponytails, a few Mohawks, shaved heads, and lots of tattoos and interesting body piercings. Even on a couple of the fiftysomethings.

Self-expression was key. Works for me. I am my dad's different drummer daughter after all.

This megachurch revolved around music. The weekend concerts attracted kids that would not normally set foot in church. No hymns, mostly variations on a theme of rock. Belatedly, I was getting into some rock music. Christian rock. I drew the line at heavy metal.

In time I became part of the singles leadership team social committee, which was a good fit for my Type A, take-charge, must-be-in-control personality. We set up mixers, barbecues, game nights, movie nights, and all manner of social events. My social committee girlfriends and I were the Cyndi Lauper poster girls for having fun.

Good clean fun, of course, since we were a church group.

Our singles social group was not just social. We helped in the community too—singing Christmas carols at nursing homes, volunteering at the emergency shelter for abused and neglected children, and sharing a picnic lunch with the homeless and passing out come-to-Jesus tracts with dessert.

I also helped lead prayer time when we broke into small groups on Friday nights. As one of the prayer leaders, it was my job to open and close prayer time and to take charge if the prayers went too long or veered off track. (Like the man who prayed about struggling with sexual sin and got a little too R-rated for our G-rated group.)

Sex was taboo for singles. Good Christians did not have sex before marriage, even those in their thirties, forties, and fifties. Everyone knew that Biblical command, and most (many) single evangelicals followed that celibate rule. Or tried to. I know I did.

To help maintain my born-again celibacy, I made up a list of not-too-radical rules for physical contact with the opposite sex: no back rubs (a.k.a. Christian sex), no handholding (*way* too romantic), no kissing until an engagement, and if you touch my ankle, you'd better marry me. (Bet you didn't know the ankle was an erogenous zone, did you?)

Purity was everything. Long before the high school purity ring craze.

The church placed a big emphasis on sex, and singles not having sex was an even bigger emphasis. Abstinence was the only letter "A" that good single Christian women should wear on their modest turtlenecks above their hearts. Purity was preached from the pulpit, as was dating, or rather the inappropriate focus on dating.

One Sunday the married senior pastor, who had obviously forgotten what it was like to be single, challenged the unmarried men in the congregation, "Do you come to church to worship God or to meet women?"

Do the two have to be mutually exclusive? Should they go to a bar to meet women instead? That always turns out so well.

I met a man at the Tuesday night Bible study who reminded me of Jesus. If Jesus had been short and wore glasses. This man was kind, gentle, and caring, with brown hair and a beard. He oozed love-thy-neighbor compassion and help for the hurting as he preached to his flock. And he *read*! His office overflowed with books. Be still my bookworm heart.

The bookish Pastor Steve was everything a good Christian woman could want in a man. Consequently, many of the women at church wanted him. Including me. I would go home after every Tuesday night Bible study to pray and write in my journal:

What is this I'm feeling for Pastor Steve?
God, is Pastor Steve the reason you brought me to this church?
Do you want Pastor Steve to become the father of my children?

Pastor Steve was well known for his great counseling skills —another plus in his favor. If we got together, I would save a ton on therapy.

I didn't save that ton, but I did meet many other men at our singles group. For the first time in my bad-relationships-with-men life, I learned what it was like to have male friends. Platonic, straight male friends. My therapist said that was a good thing. (After Paul dumped me and the-thing-that-must-not-be-named resurfaced in my memories—avalanching in feelings of shame, ugliness, and unworthiness—I had started seeing a counselor.) The problem with my new platonic male friends was I fell for a couple of them. They did not fall for me.

There was one man I was convinced was "God's will" for my life. As a Christian, it is important always to seek God's will, which is often shown through signs and wonders. "Scott" had many wonders. He was fun and easygoing. Tall. Dark. Cute. Smart. Well-read. A former missionary. *And* a Norwegian from Wisconsin. Just like me. It was clear Scott was God's will for my life.

Not to Scott. He could not see that we were made for each other. I tried to help him see. Wherever he went, I went. Like Ruth and Naomi in the Bible. *Whither thou goest...* Not in a creepy stalker way. Always in a group.

Christian singles do everything in a group. Camping, hiking, rafting, all manner of outdoorsy things, which is tricky for an indoorsy girl like me, but I sacrificed my natural inclination to fit in with the group. Mostly to fit in with Scott. I even went backpacking. Once. Squatting in the woods and using a plastic shovel to pack my poop in the ground is not my idea of a good time. I don't care how cute or how Norwegian he is. Yet

I still wanted to date Scott. Or Dan. Jake. Roy. Steve. Just about any man from my singles group. But none of them ever asked me out. Maybe it's because I reeked of desperation like a cheap perfume.

During my desperate and dateless church singles leadership days.

I enjoyed doing fun things as a group: potlucks, game nights, movie nights, scavenger hunts. But when the fun was over, I always went home alone, where many nights I cried myself to sleep. The longing to be held and loved was a physical ache, but I tried not to focus on that. I tried to focus on the spiritual, and helping others, and church.

Politics was a big focus at our megachurch.

I have always been one of the most apolitical people on the planet. Like that old stadium chant, "Lean to the left, lean to the right, stand up, sit down, fight, fight, fight," I've always leaned a little more to the left. But I didn't go to church to hear about politics; I went to church to worship God and be part of a community.

Once, before a major election, the church had a table in the lobby with voting guides, so the congregation would know how to vote the "right" way. Politically minded church volunteers staffed the table, eager to explain the ballot measures and the evangelical stance on them. I walked right on by, but several of my conservative singles friends kept pushing the pamphlets at me so I would make the right decision come Election Day.

Thanks for giving me my opinions. Saves me the trouble of thinking for myself. When did Christianity get so tied up with politics? Dietrich Bonhoeffer said politics are not the task of the Christian.

Preach it, brother.

One night I attended a Tony Campolo Crusade with a few of my singles friends. Tony, a nationally known white Baptist preacher of a predominantly black church in Philadelphia, beamed out love and goodwill to the crowd as he said, "Jesus wasn't a Republican or a Democrat." In fact, he said that to him, Jesus had always seemed more like a Democrat than a Republican with his love of the poor and disenfranchised and emphasis on taking care of the needy. Then he took an offering for AIDs patients, whom he called the lepers of the day. In the mid-eighties when AIDS hysteria was at its peak and cars sported the bumper sticker, "AIDS is God's punishment on homosexuals."

Tony was my kind of Christian. A what-would-Jesus-do kind of Christian before WWJD became part of the lexicon. But when I told my fundamentalist Christian friends how much I liked Tony and what he had to say, they raised their dogmatic eyebrows and said, "Well, you know his theology is off..."

Really?

Other evangelical friends were anti–Billy Graham because his theology was off too.

Billy Graham?

Yes. He consorted with Democrats, and God knows there are no Democrats in the evangelical church. Or if there were, they kept it on the down-low back in the day. The Democrats and the liberal media were the enemy.

When I told one of the singles guys at our Friday night group that I had returned to college to study journalism, he said, "Good! Now you can get our viewpoint across to counteract that left-wing liberal media agenda."

Silly me. Here I thought journalists were supposed to be objective. Show both sides of the story. Not give an opinion or bias unless they write an editorial. Color me naïve. Besides, why did he automatically assume I was a conservative right-wing Republican just like him?

Because we attended the same evangelical church.

During my days as a student journalist, I was assigned to cover an abortion protest. When I arrived at the outdoor venue, I found a huge, angry crowd with the large pro-life contingent on one side and the smaller pro-choice group on the other. Each side was waving signs and yelling at the other. You could cut the vitriol with a knife.

The pro-life, anti-abortion side consisted of mostly evangelical Christians. I recognized many of them from church and other Christian gatherings I had attended. These Christians, the same ones I sat next to in folding chairs on Sunday, who raised their hands in worshipful praise and adoration to God, were using those same hands to thrust signs with graphic pictures of aborted fetuses under the noses of the pro-choice crowd, their faces contorted in hate as they screamed, "Baby killers!"

So much hate. Way to win the world for Christ.

11

SOUL MATE SLACKERS AND PMS PROPOSALS

All you need is love.
But a little chocolate now and then doesn't hurt.
—Charles Schulz

I loved my church singles group, but all the men there only wanted to be pals. I had lots of pals. Tall pals, short pals, pals who climbed on rocks. Fat pals, skinny pals, even pals with argyle socks. After nearly six years in the group and pushing thirty-four, I was ready for more than a pal.

Here's the thing: when single evangelical men think a woman is romantically interested in them and they want to make sure she understands they're "just friends," they'll give her a side-armed hug. Not full frontal, that's too much temptation. And then they'll say, "I *agape* you." *Agape*, pronounced Uh-gah-pey, is Greek for godly love.

I was *agaped* a lot.

My fundamentalist jeans were starting to chafe. I peeled off those tight jeans that no longer fit and placed a dating ad in the *Pennysaver*, the weekly circular classifieds. "Wanted: A Christian man who reads." A couple male readers answered my ad and we met for coffee, but comic books and porn were not exactly what I was going for.

A few other applicants sounded promising on the phone but not so much in person. One man, a couple decades older than he had claimed, wore an ill-fitting toupee. As we chatted at the coffeehouse, I tried not to stare as his bad rug continued slipping. I kept waiting for it to fall off into his coffee. Another guy, upon meeting me and zeroing in on my too-curvy hips and thighs, said he was looking for more of a skinny-model type. We had talked on the phone a couple times before we met and seemed pretty in sync. We loved many of the same books and he was more progressive than most of the conservative church guys I knew, so I had high hopes.

His progressiveness apparently did not extend to my thighs.

Then there was the man who confessed to not being a reader but thought a Christian would make an interesting notch on his bedpost. Eww. That exercise in dating futility wiped out my limited college bank account for the month. I had neglected to read the fine print, which said every time I called the 1-900-number to listen to the potential man of my dreams, they would charge two bucks a minute. There went my grocery money.

I gave up on dating.

A few months later, a friend invited me to the church singles retreat, but I declined. I had had enough of church, and I had definitely had enough of retreats. Especially singles ones. I was mad at God for not bringing me a man as he had promised.

Christians always say, "God told me this," and, "God told me that." While I have never heard an audible voice, God speaks to me through Scripture, prayer, and often, other people. And the message I had received loud and clear from all those sources was God would bring me a man.

He was a little slow on the delivery.

Seven long, lonely years after that fundamentalist fiancé dumped me a week before our wedding, zero was happening on the romance front. I was meeting new people at school, learning new things, and realizing there was a much wider world out there beyond the small conservative Christian cocoon I lived in.

My lack of a love connection, combined with the vastness and impersonality of the megachurch (the senior pastor didn't even know my name) and the overall political mindset, left me angry and bitter and walking away from church and all my church friends.

In time, I missed them. And God. Church, not so much.

Finally, with great reluctance and much whining, I agreed to go to the singles retreat with one of my friends, even though retreats are so not my thing. (See Chapter 14.) During that gorgeous mountain getaway, there was a talent show replete with assorted singers, a band, and silly skits.

Near the end of the show, a hot guy with dark hair and a neatly trimmed beard walked onstage holding what appeared to be a baby wrapped in swaddling clothes. As Joseph, the father of Jesus, he softly crooned to that sleeping baby in his arms with much love and tenderness. Then he raised his eyes to heaven and beseeched God to show him how to be a father and raise a king.

The hard, angry shell I'd grown over my heart cracked, and I began to weep.

Afterwards, I went to thank the sensitive bearded man for cracking that hard shell around my heart, but a bunch of groupies surrounded him, vying for his attention. I retreated.

Two months later my friend "Luke" told me about a man I "just had to meet" since we had so much in common. Luke told the man the same thing about me. That man turned out to be the sensitive, bearded singer from the retreat.

Michael was different from any man I had known. Kind. Smart. Fun. Cultured. An artist with a capital A. And freakishly talented in many areas. He *quilted* for God's sake.

On our second date, I firmly declared, "I'm not giving up my writing for any man and I refuse to sew."

"That's okay, I sew."

Well, all righty then. His quilting and sewing briefly gave me pause, but then I remembered Rosey Grier, the famous football player who did needlepoint and knitting, and I relaxed. Michael also sang, acted, did woodworking, painted, and best of all: pursued me. After all those years spent running after men, it was a welcome change to be the one chased.

My first Valentine's Day with Michael came a mere two weeks after we had started dating. I was now thirty-four and living in a small mother-in-law cottage in the back of a house near the college while I wrapped up my journalism degree. That morning I was running late and rushed outside with my heavy backpack. As I approached my car, I saw it wrapped in something white.

Great, I thought. *The neighborhood kids TP'd my car.*

It wasn't toilet paper. It was a thirty-foot banner that said, *Happy Valentine's Day!* The man really knew how to score mushy points.

Later that same day when I returned home from class, I found a small piece of masking tape with a red arrow pointing right taped to my front door. I turned right and discovered another red arrow on another piece of tape. And another. And another. I followed this red-tape paper trail around to the side of my rental cottage to the outdoor utility room. Inside was a bouquet of eleven pink tulips and one red one next to a heart-shaped tin full of chocolates.

Serious mush-factor kicking in now. Hesitantly, I opened the oversized card, afraid I might find the L-word inside. It was too soon for talk of love. Thankfully, he realized that and there was no L-word. I was not quite ready for love, but I did love his wooing me. He scored some big-time, mushy brownie points that day.

That night when Michael came to pick me up, I opened the door to my beaming date, who was clad in fire engine red pants, a blue button-down Oxford shirt, and a red bow tie with white hearts. Luckily, we were going to a movie in a dark theater. As we walked to his car, I gave myself a stern internal talking-to.

Stop being so shallow. Clothes do not make the man. No man has ever been as sweet or attentive to you as this man has. Are you going to let a little thing like his wardrobe mess up your evening? Suck it up and have a good time.

Just don't look down.

Michael is not cut from the same cloth as other men. For which I am grateful. Three weeks after our first date, he told me he was in love with me.

"You're not in love," I said. "You're just infatuated."

"Call it whatever you like, but I'm that."

"You can't be in love. You don't know me well enough. There are things you don't know about me. Things you won't like."

I took a deep, scary breath and told him about my "bad-girl" *Looking for Mr. Goodbar* days. (For those under forty, *Goodbar* was a 1977 cautionary film starring Diane Keaton as a good girl who moves to New York after a painful heartbreak and starts leading a double life. By day, she is the kind, good-girl teacher of deaf children, but after dark she picks up men at bars for sex and excitement, never letting them spend the night. Until the night it all goes horribly wrong.)

I used to pick up men too. It was important for me to be the one in control and making the choice. Not them. I never let them spend the night either. I needed to wake up alone and pure in my narrow Doris Day good-girl bed. Luckily, none of my pick-ups (SPOILER ALERT) ended in death as in the movie based on a true story.

There was one terrifying time when a guy I met at a party, a quasi-local celebrity, drunkenly put his thick hands around my neck when we were making out and began to squeeze, smiling as he did so. I managed to talk my way out of that scary situation by treating it as a joke. I laughingly reminded him that everyone had seen us together and if anything happened to me, everyone would know he did it, and his budding musical career would go down the toilet. The "celebrity" gave me a drunken leer, removed his hands, and passed out, pinning my chest beneath his heavy arm. I stayed awake all night, my hatred for him increasing with each passing hour.

The next night when I was safely back in my own narrow bed again, the Nazis-chasing-me-nightmare recurred stronger and more vividly than ever.

I have never been big on digging deep beneath the surface. Lots of ugly, scary things found there. I never thought too much about the Nazi dream or examined why I kept having it. I assumed it was a side effect from living in Germany, the visit to Dachau, and all the World War II movies I watched and books I read, including Anne Frank's *The Diary of a Young Girl*.

Years later, I read an article about the meaning of dreams that said being chased usually means you are avoiding something in your waking life, or you are afraid something from your past might catch up with you.

Major lightbulb flash.

After I warned Michael about my *Mr. Goodbar* days, he said, "Doesn't matter. That's all in the past."

"It's a pretty colorful past. And there may be lasting reper-cussions."

I had been celibate for a few years, but I was concerned my sexy past might catch up with me, and I knew there was some-thing difficult I needed to do. Something I should have done a while ago. Something that terrified me. Something I knew would send this good Christian man—a man who had waited for his bride—running.

I took a deep breath and rushed out the words. "I need to get tested for AIDS. If I find out I'm HIV-positive that will be the end of this relationship."

"No, it won't." Michael took my hand and looked at me with eyes brimming with love and tenderness. "I love you. *All* of you. If you have AIDS, that is a part of you. A part of the woman I love. We will just have to work around it. And make some adjustments."

That's when I fell.

Three weeks later, Michael proposed during a PMS attack. After my hormonal meltdown, he still wanted to spend the rest of his life with me. Like Colin Firth in *Bridget Jones's Diary*, Michael likes me—loves me—just as I am. Except when I nag.

Five months after he proposed, we got married. Michael sang his vows to me. He gazed deeply into my eyes with the same love and tenderness he had shown the baby Jesus at the talent show (which I learned had been a stuffed monkey in a blanket) and the whole church, including the pastor and all the groomsmen, cried.

Within the small church we attended, there was a contin-gent of conservative couples that had discovered the writings of a former feminist who had seen the fundamentalist light and was now proclaiming the mandate for all married women to stay home, be under the "authority" of their husbands, and produce children. Procreation was the only Biblical purpose for sex, she said. Anything other than that was a perversion.

Bride and groom enjoying the gorgeous wedding cake made by my new sister-in-law, Debbie.

Children were a blessing from above; therefore, any form of birth control, even natural family planning, was wrong. Her adherents faithfully followed the Psalm, "Like arrows in the hands of a warrior are children born in one's youth. Blessed is the man whose quiver is full of them."

Having a quiver full was de rigueur for married couples, and many families in our little church subscribed to that philosophy. Several couples had six or seven children; others had eight, nine, even ten kids. (Nearly twenty years before the Duggars and *19 Kids and Counting*.)

Michael and I were such slackers.

Our beloved pastor and his sweet wife, who had several children of their own, did not subscribe to this belief, nor was it a matter of church doctrine. But it was a prevailing attitude among many couples in the church. Some of those quiver-full couples regarded us with suspicion since we had not jumped on the birthing bandwagon yet. We were still in the honeymoon phase of our marriage and in no rush to decide whether to have kids. (I had changed my long-time stance on kids and white picket fences. With Michael, I could see myself happily embracing both.)

Then the decision was made for us.

12

BOOBS, T-REX, AND EMPTY QUIVERS

*Scientists now believe that the primary biological function
of breasts is to make males stupid.*
—Dave Barry

The day after my first wedding anniversary, I was diagnosed with breast cancer. At thirty-five. After finally graduating from college and finding the love of my life, the love I did not deserve. The love I had been longing and searching for ever since my dad died. The talented, creative soulmate who told me he had always wanted to marry a fellow artist. My Renaissance man—so much better and more suited to me than my John Wayne fantasies—who accepted and loved me unconditionally, encouraged my dreams, and did not feel threatened by my feminist sensibilities.

Was my happily ever after going to end before it even began?

One week later, I had a mastectomy. I didn't care about my breast; I cared about cutting out the cancer. When Michael first saw my mastectomy scar, he kissed it tenderly and said, "I love this scar because it means I'm going to have you with me for a long time."

Please, God.

The doctors hoped they had caught my cancer early and it was only Stage One, but it turned out I had an aggressive form of breast cancer that had already spread to my lymph nodes, bumping it up to Stage Two. I was determined to fight the cancer aggressively, which is why I chose to undergo a new, experimental protocol with high doses of chemotherapy in a shorter period than usual.

The chemo kicked my butt. I have never retched so much in my entire life. I couldn't keep anything down except ice chips and sips of chicken bouillon. The very smell of food and coffee made me barf. (I hate both the taste and smell of coffee. Always have, always will.)

The nurse said it was the highest dose of chemo she had ever given a patient. Unfortunately, one of her fellow nurses forgot to give me my anti-nausea medication before they introduced the toxic chemotherapy drugs into my system for the first time.

Big mistake. *Big.*

Less than twelve hours later, I began puking my guts out. Loudly. I sounded like the T-Rex from *Jurassic Park.*

During my second chemo treatment, I retched so violently and so often, I burst the blood vessels in both my eyes. Pretty.

I lost all my hair too. There went my shot at being a Breck girl. Every single hair on my body, even eyelashes and eyebrows.

One of the worst things about having cancer was the control it had over me. I hated feeling powerless and not being in control of my own body. I didn't realize it at the time, but now I can see that subconsciously I was reacting against the-thing-that-must-not-be-named.

I may not have been able to prevent the cancer from invading my body, just as I could not prevent those frat boys from doing the same sixteen years before, but I was going to do whatever I could to exert control over this destructive attacker that is no respecter of persons.

That is why I chose to get my head buzzed when my hair first started falling out. It was my way of flipping the bird at cancer.

Confession: I have never once flipped a bird. It's not lady-like. My prissy middle finger simply will not extend itself in that universal, nonverbal symbol of harmony and goodwill. Another by-product of my etiquette-conscious mother and my prim 1960s good-girl upbringing.

Displaying my bald head a few years post chemo. Photo by Charles West.

I hadn't planned on having a boob job. I'm not a plastic-surgery kind of girl. But my mother changed my mind.

About a decade earlier when Mom was around fifty, she had breast cancer twice, resulting in two mastectomies within two years. She told me if she had been a little younger and if her insurance had covered it, she would have had reconstructive surgery. Without it, every time she dressed, she faced a daily reminder of the cancer.

I didn't want a daily reminder. I did not want cancer to control my life, so I took control and opted for reconstruction, which began in the operating room the same time as my mastectomy.

Once the plastic surgeon surgically removed my breast, she inserted a tissue expander—think a flat balloon—into my chest to stretch the tissue to make room for the saline implant that would later be inserted.

After recuperating from surgery, I went in regularly for fill-ups. My plastic surgeon filled a syringe as big as Texas with saline and pumped me up. She said I would feel "some discomfort" as the tissue expanded, but she did *not* say it would feel like I had a Frisbee jammed inside my chest.

In time, to my relief, I wound up with a perky new breast complete with a tattooed nipple.

Problem was, once I got healthy again, I regained all the weight I had lost during chemotherapy. My real breast got bigger, but my rebuilt perky one—designed when I was thirty pounds lighter—no longer matched. I had to start stuffing my bra again, something I had not done since eighth grade.

I started with toilet paper, followed it with tissues, graduated to some of Michael's quilt batting, and then shoulder pads, until I finally broke down and got a proper prosthesis. Silicone, complete with simulated nipple.

I loved my new breast form so much I wore it around the house on weekends … times I usually went braless.

The first Saturday I wore it, a plumber came over to replace our broken toilet. Being the clean queen I am, while he was removing the toilet bolts, I was scrubbing away vigorously at some hard water stains in the bathtub.

All at once, there was a loud SPLAT. There, balanced on the edge of the bathtub, sat my new prosthesis in all its quivering pink glory.

"Oops. Lost my breast," I said, scooping up the silicone before the plumber's bugged-out eyes. "It's new."

I have always been an optimistic and resilient person, which some people find annoying. I tend to bounce back quickly from disappointments and setbacks and try to maintain my sense of humor about most things. But some things just aren't funny.

Since I got so sick from the heavy doses of chemo, I had to be hospitalized for every treatment. Michael tried to distract me with games of cribbage and Boggle, but sometimes midgame I would have to grab the plastic basin and puke. After a while, there was nothing in my stomach to throw up, and still I kept on puking and the dry heaves kept on coming.

All I wanted to do was die. Then I was terrified I might die.

Confronting your own mortality does that. I sought comfort in the Psalms: *The cords of death entangled me; the torrents of destruction overwhelmed me...In my distress I called to the Lord; I cried to my God for help...He reached down from on high and took hold of me...He rescued me from my powerful enemy...*

I clung to the word *rescue* like a life preserver, and the terror subsided. Peace replaced the fear. Cancer might claim my body, but it could never claim my soul.

My soulmate was by my side every step of my cancer journey. Michael held the bucket when I threw up. Gave me shots to bring my white blood cell count back up to normal. Kept track of my medications and when I was supposed to receive them (so there would not be a repeat of the anti-nausea med fiasco), and caressed my billiard-ball head while telling me I was beautiful. When my oncologist prescribed home health care and hydration after each hospitalization, the home health nurse showed my beloved how to change the IV bags of saline and administer my anti-nausea medication, which came in a lightweight, clear plastic oval the size of a baseball.

My artsy-craftsy husband saved those empty "chemo balls" to turn into Christmas ornaments. He's big on recycling. The truth is, Michael is a sentimental guy who likes souvenirs as a remembrance of places we've gone, things we've done, and significant moments in our life. So, every year (except the first, the cancer was still too fresh, and I did not want a reminder of the horrible chemo days) we unpack our His 'n' Her chemo ball ornaments and hang them on the Christmas tree to mark another year cancer-free. This Christmas, it will be thirty years. Thank God.

When we asked my kindly oncologist if the cancer could affect the possibility of our having children, something we still had not decided upon, he advised us that having a child could take years off my life. He suggested if we did decide to have kids that we wait at least five years in case any lingering cancer cells remained. That way the pregnancy hormones would not cause the cancer cells to grow and spread.

In five years, I would be in my early forties, which we both agreed at that time was a little old (for us) to start having kids. The doctor's recommendation confirmed our on-the-fence decision. My Renaissance man said he would get a vasectomy so we would not run the risk of my getting pregnant. I suggested I get a hysterectomy instead. That way if I died, he could still have children.

"Your dying is not an option," Michael said, adding that he was not about to put my poor, beleaguered body through any additional trauma.

I did not want to deprive my beloved of the chance to have children; he did not want to deprive me of the chance to have life.

When we returned to church after my cancer surgery, our empty quiver was more conspicuous than ever. One of the young fruitful moms seeking to comfort me said, "Don't worry. You can still nurse with only one breast."

13

THE GOOD, THE BAD, AND THE SUPERFICIAL

I read Shakespeare and the Bible, and I can shoot dice.
That's what I call a liberal education.
—Tallulah Bankhead

Many of the quiver-full couples at our small church also subscribed to the belief advocated by the-former-feminist-turned-fundamentalist-prophet that their Christian children should all be homeschooled.

Soon the denim-jumpered home-school brigade outnumbered the rest of the church faithful. More and more, the conversations at church revolved around cloth diapers versus Pampers, homeschooling curriculum, and the evil of "the world," public schools, and anything outside of their conservative Christian bubble.

We saw the writing on the homeschooling wall and left.

After breaking free from the church of the open womb, we visited several churches of different denominations, trying to find one that was a better fit, including a couple Baptist churches. But Michael grew up in Baptist churches and was not crazy about all the rules and restrictions: no drinking, no dancing, and no divorce. Not that he was contemplating the big D-word himself.

His beloved older sister Sheri, on the other hand, who had been leading intensive Bible studies for years and was the wisest, most honest person we knew—a woman of deep moral integrity—was prohibited from ascending any higher up the church leadership ladder because her husband had been divorced years before he married her.

Bye, bye, Baptist.

We continued our church shopping. We visited small churches, large churches, Black churches, White churches, Presbyterian, Methodist, Assemblies of God, foursquare, too square, and everything in between.

I started feeling like Cinderella's shoe.

Then we visited another church with a friend who had left Christianity behind a few decades earlier. After a recent health scare, she said she wanted to get right with God and start going to church again, but she was nervous about going alone. So, we tagged along several times to her church of choice: a hip, rockin' nondenominational place of worship in an upscale suburb of town.

The pastor was a fiftyish guy in jeans and a goatee who drove a Hummer and had a colorful past, having left behind a life of booze, drugs, crime, and punishment when he came to Jesus. He laced his sermons with a blend of Bible-thumping teaching, relevance, and humor.

He lost the humor the Sunday he began preaching against Harry Potter, the books that had gotten children of all ages reading again. And which many adults, including me, devoured.

"Harry Potter is evil," he said. "Those books promote sorcery and witchcraft."

Guess he missed that whole Dumbledore being the Christ figure part.

As the goateed pastor with the criminal past railed against the evils of witchcraft, he claimed that its insidious roots in American pop culture began in 1939 when *The Wizard of Oz* with Judy Garland was released and children across the country first met a "good" witch. I think maybe that pastor had taken one too many trips over the rainbow in his BC days. He had also missed the fact that decades earlier, there was a hugely popular series of Oz books by L. Frank Baum, complete with a good witch, long before the movie.

Clearly, that pastor wasn't a reader. At least of fiction. Make-believe.

Our church search continued.

One Sunday, some friends invited us to visit their church. I was not crazy about the idea of another big-box church, but these friends had left the same too-cool-for-school megachurch that we had and reassured us that the pastor of their new church did not bang the political drum loudly. Apparently, he was also a good teacher and charismatic speaker, albeit not in the Pentecostal sense. When they mentioned that the church had an active drama and music ministry, my actor/singer husband's ears stood at attention.

We checked it out one Sunday and stayed seven years.

We loved the sermon that first Sunday, especially when the pastor said the church believed that each person was formed by God to be loved by him and that God wanted our love in return. "We believe in the sovereignty of the Word of God, and that our unity is found in Christ alone," he said. "On all other points of doctrine, we agree to disagree."

That sold us. We were so weary of all the theological debate and arguments at the other churches we had been to: Calvinism versus Arminianism, premillennial versus postmillennial, pretrib versus posttrib, end times versus the best of times, the worst of times. It was a welcome relief to find a church that did not sweat the small stuff of doctrinal differences.

We quickly immersed ourselves in our new big-box church. In addition to attending church every Sunday, we went to an adult Sunday school class, I joined a weekly women's Bible study, and Michael joined the music and drama ministry. A night-and-day difference from the former hip megachurch that rocked out on Sunday mornings, although both used drums and flashed the lyrics on large movie screens.

At our new church, the music ministry was more like Disneyland or Hollywood. And since Michael loved Disneyland and I loved Hollywood, what could be better? There was lots of glitz and razzle-dazzle, like the Busby Berkeley musicals popular in the 1930s. In addition to a full choir and a rotating series of gorgeous young vocalists with lots of teeth who sang solos on Sunday with a trio of back-up singers, there were also dancing girls who would plié down the aisles in snug, sparkly costumes and dazzling Marie Osmond smiles.

The music director would highlight holy holidays with special music and performances during Easter, Memorial Day, and the Fourth of July. Even showering the congregation with an explosion of red, white, and blue confetti on the patriotic holidays. It was like having our own Boston Pops in California. The highlight of the church year was the Christmas musical.

Talk about Disneyland.

The music director wrote an original musical each Christmas, complete with toe-tapping new songs and a come-to-Jesus plot. The basic message in the glitzy production was always the same, only the songs and setting changed yearly. That annual holiday musical was our biggest community outreach. It played to packed houses every year, drawing huge crowds from the community and resulting in hundreds of "decisions for Christ." (Translation: The pastor issued an altar call near the end of every holiday performance that hundreds answered to become born-again Christians.)

My Renaissance-man husband, who had worked in a professional theater company for a few years, was often involved with several aspects of the production. From acting, directing, and stage managing, to contributing costumes, building sets, or making props. One year he even roped me into helping him paint three-foot-tall wooden candy canes. Seventy of them.

At least he knew better than to ask me to sew.

Michael is indispensable behind the scenes, but his passion is acting. The man is a natural, gifted actor. He was thrilled when the music director told him that he had written a great dramatic role in that year's holiday musical especially for him. I was thrilled when I learned that my husband, whose beautiful tenor voice always makes my heart melt, would be singing a solo.

Michael was excited about getting a meaty role he could finally sink his acting teeth into. He knocked everyone dead at the first audition. The callback too. But the music director gave the role to someone else. Someone taller with hardly any acting experience. Someone God had "told him" to cast.

I wanted to tell the music director that God had told me to take him out.

Then he asked Michael to direct the play and coach the novice actor who stole my husband's part.

I wanted to call up that music director and tell him where he could put his script.

Michael, initially devastated, agreed to direct the show and coach the actor. "This outreach is so much bigger than any one individual," he told me. "Who am I to question who God wants in what role?"

My husband is far more spiritual than I am. I still wanted to take the director out.

The production was a success, and the tenor who replaced him did a great job singing the solo. Michael still would have acted rings around him. Just sayin'.

Most churches end their Christmas plays with the stable scene and everyone bowing down in reverence before that babe in the manger, but our glitzy musical extravaganza always continued beyond Bethlehem with at least two more production numbers. For the finale, the stage was crammed with every single cast member, all the choirs, and the ubiquitous dancing girls.

The problem was the audience never knew when it was over.

Some would start to clap at the end of the manger scene, only to be silenced by a flashy production number. When that number ended, the clapping would begin again, only to be interrupted by an even bigger and flashier production number.

Apparently, all the flash and glitz and the bigger-is-better formula worked, because we packed them in. In time, we outgrew our church stage and had to rent out a large local concert hall instead. That proved expensive, and since the church was now so popular and growing, it was decided that we needed a bigger church.

Thus, the dreaded words: building campaign. Not one of my favorite things. All those grow-your-church strategies and ghostwritten books from televangelists with lots of Colgate-white teeth who live in McMansions and drive Porsches made the skin around my WWJD bracelet crawl.

My wrist began to itch.

The itching increased as our megachurch exploded into a massive, sprawling complex, dwarfing most of the other churches in town and requiring a cop to manage traffic on Sundays. We stayed, unwilling to leave our eloquent pastor whose words so captivated us and spoke to our hearts week after week. Even when his image was now projected on three massive screens as he preached, so those in the cheap seats could see the action on stage.

The itching grew worse. For Michael, too.

He had initially enjoyed being part of the music and drama ministry, but as time went on, the church grew, and the glitz-factor increased exponentially...leaving the taste of too much glitter in our mouths. On the one-year anniversary celebration of our brand-new mega-building, they pulled out all the stops in a gala razzle-dazzle extravaganza to beat the band, complete with triple the number of dancing girls and multiple blasts of sparkly confetti from all sides that showered the audience. Um, congregation.

We looked at each other and both knew that was our last Sunday. We wanted church, not Disneyland.

14

STRIP MONOPOLY AND THE WOO-WOO FACTOR

We are not human beings having a spiritual experience; we are
spiritual beings having a human experience.
—Pierre Teilhard de Chardin

After the big Disneyland church, we yearned for something more intimate without all the flash and dash, and with more of a sense of the sacred and spiritual. Michael suggested we visit a small charismatic church, the same denomination of a humble Texas church he had belonged to when he lived in Houston.

I was hesitant to go the charismatic route because I'm not a big fan of woo-woo. You know, the out-there, mystical, off-the-wall spiritual stuff like people being "slain in the spirit," or laughing in some kind of holy ecstasy. I've inherited my dad's dreamer tendencies, but I have also inherited some of his skepticism.

My husband was more open to the expression of the "gifts of the spirit" and really wanted to go, so finally I agreed to check it out. Our first Sunday at the little urban church, two long-haired women danced barefoot before the altar during worship. Unlike any dancing I'd ever seen in church—the total opposite from the razzle-dazzle big-box church we'd just left.

At the Disneyland church, the dancing girls performed for the congregation as if they were on a Broadway stage, flashing their teeth continually at the audience in wide showgirl grins. Here, in this small charismatic church, we could not even see the faces of these two dancing women. They faced the front of the church, their backs to the congregation, gliding past the altar silently, swirling billowing scarves in a gentle motion.

My breath caught in my throat and my soul felt a stirring it had not felt in some time. At the end of their dance of worship, the women bowed before the altar in an attitude of total surrender and humility, raising their hands up to the heavens, scarves trailing, in praise and adoration to God.

Not a shred of glitz between them.

We bowed our heads too. In his sermon "The Weight of Glory", C. S. Lewis said "we do not want merely to see beauty… we want something else which can hardly be put into words: to be united with the beauty we see, to pass into it, to receive it into ourselves, to bathe in it, to become part of it." We received that beauty into ourselves, we bathed in it, and became part of it—that mystical, reverential dance of worship—and did not want to leave.

The beauty of the worship dance drew us to the charismatic urban church made up of mostly young people with only a handful of folks in their forties, like us. But it was the way the church members reached out to the poor and homeless and welcomed them into the church that kept us there.

The church also stressed the importance of small groups like the early church in the book of Acts, so we started a small group in our home. Rather than inviting only people from our new charismatic church, we also included a dozen or so friends from other places of worship, and some who did not attend church at all.

We would meet every other week to pray, talk about God and life, wrestle with issues of faith, and reflect on passages of the Bible or spiritual books we'd read. We discussed books by C. S. Lewis, Phillip Yancey, Anne Lamott, and Donald Miller. *Traveling Mercies* and *Blue Like Jazz* were favorites, but a couple of the more conservative members didn't understand why Anne felt the need to swear in her writings. Swearing wasn't very Christian.

Sheesh. That word is a favorite in much of Christian fiction. I've used it myself a few times in my fluffy Christian chick-lit novels, even though "sheesh" has never once passed my lips. But when you write for the evangelical Christian marketplace, you learn early on that censorship is part of the publishing package.

Book signing for my first book, Dated Jekyll, Married Hyde.

I discovered this during the writing of my first book, *Dated Jekyll, Married Hyde,* a humorous, lighthearted look at celebrating the differences between husbands and wives. I included a scene about Michael and I playing strip poker but was told I could not use *those words.* Knowing how sensitive many born-agains are about sex and, particularly, sex words, I was prepared to delete the word "strip."

Since I was writing for a Christian publisher and my books would be carried in Christian bookstores, I knew there was an element of censorship that took place. I had heard stories of the blue-haired gatekeepers who promptly returned a book to their favorite Christian bookstore if there was any sex, drinking, or language in it, and I understood that my publisher had to acquiesce to the gatekeepers to stay in business.

Turned out that *strip* was okay since we were married. *Poker* was the naughty word. Gambling. Good thing I hadn't written about Reno or Las Vegas. The publisher wanted to change it to strip Yahtzee, but I held out for strip Monopoly. Those go-directly-to-jail, do-not-pass-go possibilities were endless.

In my forties I belonged to a couple Christian writing groups where we had many discussions on the language in our books being sanitized to appease those bookstore gatekeepers. The prevailing attitude among most of the evangelical authors I knew was that good writers do not need to resort to profanity. There is some truth to that, but neither should writers have to resort to arcane expressions from the fifties like "golly" and "sheesh."

Reminds me of when I interviewed a group of women for my book on breast cancer. One of the women said she was "pissed off" about losing her breast. One of the advance Christian reviewers knew that the p-word would never pass muster with the language police, so suggested alternative words like "vexed."

Vexed? At having your breast sliced off?

Shades of Southern belles from times gone by, fluttering their fans and feeling vexed by the heat. I felt like Goldilocks. I simply did not fit. Thankfully, my editor stood up for the honesty of the book and the p-word remained.

Several of the editors I worked with at the different Christian publishing houses over the years chafed under the restrictions imposed by the bookstore gatekeepers. But it is what it is, so you figure out a creative way to work with it or around it.

Until it doesn't work for you anymore or fit who you've become.

The urban charismatic church wasn't a perfect fit for us either. The woo-woo factor still gave me pause. But we'd realized that no church would ever be perfect, and overall, it met our spiritual needs. And we were also able to meet the needs of others in the nearby community, which was important to us. The beauty and reverence toward worship is what really drew us to this Pentecostal church.

Sure, there was the occasional overly loud praise song as the drummer head-banged for Jesus, but as long as there was also mellow music and the spirit dancers, my easy-listening ears could cope.

After more than a year of checking out this little church that had become our Sunday home, we decided it was time to get more involved. The day they had Ministry Sunday, we decided to join one of the ministries and start serving others instead of just taking up folding-chair space.

We considered hospitality, since we have always been good at entertaining, but wanted something a little deeper than serving coffee and cookies. We bypassed the healing ministry because I knew it would be way too far out on the fringe for my anti-woo-woo sensibilities. At last, we decided on the prayer ministry since we liked praying for others. I also thought it would be a bit more innocuous than some of the other options provided.

I got that wrong.

The duo in charge of the prayer ministry had us all stand in a circle as they explained to our group of eight what would be required of us as members of the prayer team. They said it would be a good idea to do a two-team approach, as in one of us should stand behind the other to catch them in case they fell out.

Fell out?

Then they began to pray. And one by one, each potential prayer-team member within the circle "fell out" in the spirit, except Michael and me.

We opted to serve in the coffee hour ministry instead.

There were many things about this little church that I liked, even loved, so I tried to let the out-there Pentecostal aspects of it slide. Like speaking in tongues and people giving us "words of knowledge," or prophesying. Until one Sunday after service when I was at the back of the church talking to a girlfriend. Suddenly we heard this loud voice yell, "Get out!"

"Uh, that's your husband he's talking to." My friend inclined her head toward the front of the church.

I whirled around in time to see one of the overly zealous young men laying his hands on Michael, who had gone forward for prayer for a health issue. The young guy kept shouting, "Get out!" Finally, I realized he was trying to cast a demon out of my beloved.

We were so outta there.

Someone tried to cast a demon out of me once in my early evangelical days. When I first came to faith, there were still some problem areas in my life that I struggled with. Things "good Christian girls" did not/should not do.

Even alone in their bedroom.

As a brand-new virgin-in-Christ, I felt guilty raising my hand in praise and adoration to God with the same hand I used for nocturnal delights. I knew I needed to be cleansed and set free from this bad ("dirty") habit. I was too embarrassed to reveal the specific problem I was struggling with, so some evangelical friends suggested I visit a friend of theirs with a "deliverance" ministry that might help.

Burt Reynolds and banjo music filled my head.

Thankfully, there were no signs of Burt when I went to see Joan one hot summer afternoon. I liked Joan right away. She was blunt, passionate, funny, and sincerely wanted to help Christians break free from bonds that were oppressing them. Bonds that she believed were demonic.

I shared my sinful struggle with her, and she grabbed my hands in hers, closed her eyes, and began to pray fervently. In tongues. For an hour.

Well, ten minutes that felt like an hour.

I prayed too, but quietly. She continued praying in tongues, saying the same words repeatedly and squeezing my hands tightly. My nose itched, but I could not scratch it because she held my hands captive in hers. Then her praying grew louder and more intense. "Come out of her, come out," she said. Joan repeated the command several times, alternating it with tongues and snippets of Scripture.

The minutes ticked on. Now my nose was seriously itching, and I really needed to scratch it.

My foot was falling asleep. My throat was dry. And sweat was trickling down my T-shirt. I felt sticky and icky and longed for nothing more than a long shower and a tall glass of iced tea.

Still, Joan kept praying and saying, "Come out! Come out of her!"

Then I got a tickle in my dry throat and coughed.

"Ah!" She raised our clasped hands in triumph. "Stubborn little demon, weren't you?"

After the attempted demon-casting at the little charismatic church, we gave up and stopped going to church altogether. We still kept up our small, ragtag home group and decided that would be our church instead. If it was good enough for the believers in Acts, it was good enough for us.

Then one by one, our home group members who still attended the church we had left began to drop out. Eventually, only half the group remained. Okay with us. We've always preferred intimate gatherings to big crowds, which was why we were so out of place in all the big-box churches.

There were some aspects of church I missed: the people, music, and worship most of all. I did *not* miss the woo-woo factor. Or the Christianese. That insider "us versus them" language evangelicals speak that leaves the rest of the world out in the cold.

Expressions like *backsliding, convicted, End Times, milk versus meat, testimony, the Rapture, tongues, walking your talk, unequally yoked, secular,* and the *Proverbs 31 woman.*

The latter set the bar for what many fundamentalist Christian men wanted in a wife—including my first fiancé. Someone who could spin wool and flax, make her own bedspreads, plant a vineyard, and get up before dawn to make breakfast for her household. The breakfast part I've got down cold (I make some mean scrambled eggs), but the rest, not so much.

No wonder he dumped me.

Another plus to not going to church was sleeping in on Sunday mornings. Michael and I got in the habit of enjoying a leisurely breakfast together, puttering around in the yard, and taking our dog for long walks through the neighborhood. Other times we would go out to brunch with our non-churchy friends, or go to the first Sunday matinee, the cheapest movie of the day that we had always missed before. Some Sundays we would take a drive in the country where we would worship at the altar of wildflowers, mountains, or the sea.

The ocean has always had restorative powers for me. As I walk barefoot along the edge of the shore, the salt water from the incoming waves washes across my feet, purifying my weary, callused soles. And soul. We would explore the beach and find smooth, worn pebbles, sand dollars, and sea glass. I would sit in the sand for hours reading or staring out to sea while Michael flew his kite, my worries and concerns soothed by the crashing of the waves and the sound of the wind.

Carried out to sea and released.

In Genesis, it says, "and the spirit of God moved upon the face of the waters." I could sense God's spirit moving whenever I faced the waters.

Recently I discovered a 1984 journal entry where I wrote:

I walk toward the pounding surf, the waves inexorably beckoning me closer. It seems as if I could just continue walking right into the sea and the waves would gently carry me away to a far-off magical land...The vastness of sea and sky meeting to become one. Woman, the sky, golden and radiant; man, the sea, forceful and pounding, merging into oneness . . .

Clearly written during my celibate period.

15

SINATRA, NECK SLUTS, AND BAD EVANGELICALS

In the course of my life, I have often had to eat my words,
and I must confess that I have always found it a wholesome diet.
—Winston Churchill

I was not a very good evangelical.

I never quite fit the conservative fundamentalist mold. Except for that four-or-five-year-period in my early fundie days when I was prim, proper, and judgy of others who did not toe the evangelical church line. Especially when it came to purity. (My judginess had nothing to do with the sexual baggage from my former life and the-thing-that-must-not-be-named.)

"You're wearing *that?*" I would say, arching an eyebrow above my bangs. "Not very modest. You might want to change so you don't make the single men stumble." "Stumble" is a favorite Christianese expression. Definition: fall into sin.

"You were alone in a hotel room with a man for five minutes picking up brochures for the conference? Way to watch that whole appearance of evil thing."

"You let him kiss you on the third date?"

"Slut."

I know a slut when I see one because I was a neck slut with Michael. On our second date, no less. We were being a good evangelical Christian couple and getting to know each other without physical contact confusing our budding romantic relationship.

We had had a picnic on the beach and spent hours walking, talking, listening to music, and quizzing each other on movie trivia, since we are both die-hard movie lovers. (I won, but that's not important.) All day long as I breathed in the sea air, I had been longing for this gorgeous, bearded man to hold my hand. Put his arm around me. *Something.* But Michael was being a stalwart bastion of evangelical purity and dating boundaries, which made me yearn for him even more.

I was not about to make a move. Even if I was feeling romantic and yearny, and it was difficult to tamp down my take-charge, in control, Diana-the-huntress personality and not grab him in a lip-lock. I was done with chasing men. This time, I wanted a man to chase *me.*

Then I blew it. On the two-hour drive home, as we were talking and listening to music, all of a sudden, my left hand reached up of its own volition and began massaging the back of Michael's neck.

Neck slut. I blame it on Sinatra.

I couldn't believe what I had done. What had come over me? I was following in President Jimmy Carter's footsteps, who had admitted years before in that famous *Playboy* interview that he had lusted in his heart. My lust had just extended a little higher. I'd broken the essential evangelical Christian purity rules and my own decree about not being aggressive or taking the lead in the relationship. Michael was bound to bolt for the hills in horror.

After all, what good Christian man wants to date a neck slut?

Thankfully, Michael did not hold my forward, feminist, lusty behavior against me. On our next date, he held my hand. We both toed the good evangelical line back then.

One evangelical line I never toed was retreats.

I am so not a retreat girl. Christian women love their group spiritual retreats. What's not to love? A bunch of women crowded together in the great outdoors in rustic cabins with bugs, bare-bones bunk beds, uncomfortable mattresses bearing the dead skin of hundreds of campers who came before, a surfeit of junk food, goofy games, and a dozen women all sharing the same bathroom.

Where do I go to sign up?

The worst retreat I attended was an out-of-state weekend singles retreat a few years into my marriage when I was still deep into my fundie stage. The singles leadership team had booked me as their keynote speaker after reading one of my humor books on Christian singlehood and dating disasters. Disliking retreats as I do, particularly with strangers, I was hesitant to accept, but we were short on cash and a weekend speaking gig brought in a nice chunk of change, so I overcame my reluctance.

The first clue I had that it was going to be a bad weekend came when two of the leaders picked me up at the airport—an attractive, fortyish blonde woman and a forty-something man with a graying ponytail. As the man stowed my suitcase in the back of the SUV, he winked at me and inclined his head to a rolled-up bundle in the corner.

"That's your sleeping bag," he said. "We know how much you like roughing it."

It went downhill from there.

As the leaders talked during the two-hour drive to the retreat campground, I learned they were dating. As they

continued to talk, I realized to my mounting good-girl fundamentalist horror that this single, UNMARRIED couple was
sleeping together. In clear, unadulterated sin. Ponytail man
shared how their pastor preached it was unreasonable to
expect celibacy of divorced singles in their thirties and forties.

He must have read a different Bible than me.

I could not wait to get out of their sex van. When we
arrived at the campground, ponytail man handed me the extra
sleeping bag. *Eww, what if they had had sex in that bag?*

That evening at dinner, as I met and talked to the other
singles, it was clear that most of them shared the same sinful
sex-before-marriage-is-okay attitude. What kind of church did
they attend? Church of the Open Fornication?

I felt like Pollyanna in Sodom and Gomorrah.

My first talk came after dinner, where I shared anecdotes
from my Christian singles days that the audience identified
with and laughed at. Afterwards, we gathered around the
campfire for fellowship and s'mores. I assumed the group
would do the standard Christian singles retreat thing, pull out
a guitar and sing praise songs or share Scripture and testi-
monies. Instead, someone pulled out some wine, someone else
told a risqué joke, and I grew more and more uncomfortable.

Excusing myself, I said I was tired and needed an early
night. Back at the retreat cabin, I sought prayer and counsel
from the sweet, retired missionary couple in their eighties who
had been invited along as token chaperones.

The elderly couple was as uncomfortable as I was by the
obvious sin and "worldly" attitudes of much of the group. They
advised me that since I was the designated speaker, it was *my*
duty to call the singles into account for their sinful behavior.

Me? The good girl who hates conflict.

I'm just the funny speaker from out of town. I'm no Bible
teacher or pastor. It would be much better coming from them
since they attended the same church, had the benefit of years

and wisdom on their side, and as missionaries, they were the *anointed*. But the older couple was adamant that as the weekend speaker, and therefore, leader, it was my responsibility to confront the sin in our midst.

Great. I'm far away from home in a different state. Stuck in a rustic cabin in the middle of nowhere with a bunch of sex-crazed single strangers. My only transportation out of there? The sinning couple I am supposed to confront the next day.

Where do I go to turn in my evangelical speakers' circuit card?

I stayed up most of the night, rewriting my notes, feeling nauseous, and longing for some tequila. By four in the morning, I couldn't keep my eyes open any longer. Pulling on extra layers of clothes, I crawled into my uncomfortable bunk bed, teeth chattering in the cold. No way was I going to burrow down inside the germ-ridden sleeping bag they'd provided. After freezing for a bit, I decided I didn't want to die of exposure either. I unrolled the sleeping bag and pulled it over me like a quilt, taking care not to touch the insides of the germy sex bag.

Anxious about confronting the sinning couple driving me back to the airport the next day, I opted to take the coward's way out. I decided to casually weave in multiple scriptures against fornication amongst my own tales of Christian purity, making it funny, of course, to soften the implied rebuke. If I confronted them directly, I was worried the Sodom-and-Gomorrah couple might leave me stranded on the side of the road in the middle of nowhere. Or worse, smother me with their sex sleeping bags in their orgy van, cut my confrontational body into tiny pieces, and bury me in the desert where scavenging coyotes would sniff out, dig up, and eat my judgmental remains.

My coward's talk went over like a pig on Passover.

And people wonder why I do not like retreats.

Part of the problem is I am not a nature girl. I love the idea of nature and the beauty of nature. Spring is my favorite season, when everything begins to bloom in a dizzying array of scents and colors—cherry blossoms, camellias, daffodils, daisies, and roses everywhere. The reality of nature? Not so much. Too many creepy crawlers and nasty critters, who do not talk or sing like Disney cartoon animals.

I am a woman who needs her creature comforts. Yet occasionally I am willing to sacrifice them for the greater good.

Like the times in my mid-forties when I went with my girl-friend Jan to her rustic summer cabin in the woods for weekend writing getaways when I was on a book deadline. Without the distractions of home, husband, dog, and email, I could usually whip out three or four first-draft chapters for my humor books in a day, rather than a month.

The first time I went to the cabin, it was spring. As country-girl Jan unlocked the front door, she said casually over her shoulder to suburbs-girl me, "Don't be surprised if we find a dead critter or two inside."

"A dead critter?" I vaulted backward three feet.

"Just a mouse or a lizard."

Mouse? As in *rodent*? As in from the same family as my mortal enemy, rats?

"They come in during the winter to get warm."

"But how do they get in if the door's locked?" I asked in a quavering voice.

Our cabin writeaways were always a peaceful, productive time. During another writing getaway in November, we'd had an especially productive day, so celebrated with dinner and an old black-and-white tearjerker on VHS. It was a nice, lazy evening, and around midnight, we were winding down to go to bed when we heard voices outside. Followed by heavy feet pounding across the back deck. Directly behind me. Followed by a loud banging on the back door.

We jumped off our respective couches.

Jan grabbed the nearby axe that she had used to chop firewood earlier and tentatively approached the flimsy back door. "Who is it? What do you want?" she yelled.

"It's an emergency," a female voice yelled back from the other side of the door. A door I now noticed (to my mounting, mindless terror) was *unlocked*. "There's a big ol' fire nearby."

"Jan," I hissed, "call the police or a neighbor."

"The police would take twenty minutes to get here," she hissed back. "Besides, there are no neighbors around. We're the only ones out here. It's winter. Off-season."

Outside, just beyond the insubstantial hollow door, a male voice mumbled something indistinguishable to his female companion. *They were making plans to rob and kill us. I knew it.* Three female Yosemite tourists had been tortured and killed in the general vicinity a few years earlier in a horrible murder that made national headlines. Jan had casually mentioned the night before that the authorities had found the murdered women's burned car and bodies nearby.

I inched over to the back door, shaking all the way, and quietly locked it. Now we were mostly safe. (But I knew it would not take much for our unwanted visitors to break down the feeble door if they really wanted to.)

Jan, still clutching the axe, yelled back to the pretending-to-be-good-Samaritans duo, "Thanks for letting us know. We're fine. We'll call the fire department."

"Oh...okay," said the woman. Then the two—at least we think it was two; it could have been five, ten, even fifteen—strangers clomped away. Moments later, we heard a truck start up and spin down the snow-packed dirt road. Meanwhile, Jan was furiously phoning the police and forest service to tell them what had happened.

I waited a few minutes until I was sure the murderous Samaritan truckers were gone and peeked out the front window. I could not see anything. Not even stars. The words *pitch-black* took on a completely new meaning. The darkness was absolute and all-encompassing on that overcast night in the lonely winter woods.

Trembling uncontrollably, I started throwing clothes in my suitcase. "We need to get out of here before they come back," I squeaked as Jan hung up the phone.

"I don't think they'll be back. The Forest Service said they have dozens of brush clean-up fires burning in the area—the normal stuff they do every year. That couple was just trying to warn us."

"Maybe, maybe not." I yanked open the fridge and started tossing perishables into the ice chest. "But I can't stay here tonight. I did not realize how isolated and vulnerable we were out here. There is no one close by if we need help—"

The phone rang, interrupting my hysterics.

Jan answered and listened to the voice on the other end of the line. "They did? Okay, thanks." She hung up. "That was the sheriff's department. They said a couple that lives in the area just called and told them they had stopped by to warn us about the fire. They were just being good neighbors."

"Maybe." I continued my frenzied packing. "Or *maybe* they called the sheriff's office to prevent them from coming out and checking on us. Once they know the coast is clear, they'll be back to torture and murder us and make off with our laptops."

Jan lifted an eyebrow. "Do you think maybe you read too many mysteries?"

"Possibly." I gave her a weak smile to acknowledge that I knew I was overreacting. "But I'm still not staying here tonight. Let's go to the nearest town and find a nice, safe motel. I'll pay."

Realizing how terrified I was, my friend graciously acquiesced. Yet for some reason she has not invited me back for another writing getaway. I doubt my thrashing legs in bed all night as I ran away from the Nazis during my recurring nightmare that I hadn't had in years had anything to do with it.

Later, when I was able to think about it rationally, I realized my fear was not so much about being a girl of the suburbs but rather a lingering side effect of the-thing-that-must-not-be-named. I thought I had closed the door on that traumatic event and "gotten over it" ages ago. Yet finding myself in an isolated, off-season area with no one around, and a flimsy door as the only protection between us and a potential gang of hulking men waiting to overpower and assault us, triggered flashbacks of that night and stirred up age-old, deep-seated fears.

FEAR AND LOATHING IN CALIFORNIA

*Fear is the brain's way of saying that there is
something important for you to overcome.*
—Rachel Huber

I t wasn't only my fears that were stirred up by flashbacks
of that awful night; it was also anger, which occasionally
bubbled up and out at unexpected times.

Like book club.

Michael and I had started a coed book club in our home
several years before. The intent was to keep things fun and
light by reading mainstream fiction, uplifting memoirs and
biographies, and beloved classics. We did *not* want to read
anything too dark, heavy, or deep.

Call us shallow, but at the time, after suffering some devas-
tating losses, we needed an escape. To be swept away by a good
story. We wanted to read for pleasure and entertainment, not a
college English class. We even told our dear friend Shane, a
spiritual, intellectual man who prefers dark and deep and does
not read commercial fiction, that we were intentionally *not*

inviting him to the club since we knew our book choices would not be to his more literary, esoteric tastes.

Months later, new members had joined, and we neglected to inform them of the type of books we preferred to read. Our bad.

Before long, dark, heavy, and deep had taken over, and Shane, upon hearing some of the titles, told us he would love to join the club. His first book choice was a selection of short stories by Flannery O'Connor. People had raved about Flannery for years, calling her an amazing and spiritual writer, so she had been on my mental TBR list for quite a while.

I was looking forward to finally reading this much-admired writer. It did not go well.

We read the first short story in *A Good Man Is Hard to Find*, and I hated it. Too dark and disturbing. SPOILER ALERT: I was horrified when, two-by-two, the members of an entire family, including a couple children and a *baby*, were randomly murdered. Yes, the murders occurred off the page, but still. I know there is some profound spiritual theme to this famous story that I am not digging deep enough to find, but I don't care. I cannot handle reading about or seeing innocent people being tortured or senselessly killed.

That is also why I hated the black comedy, cult-classic movie *Fargo* that so many love. Sure, as a midwestern girl with relatives still living in the Cheese State, I smiled in recognition of the familiar speech. "Yah? Oh yah. You betcha." But I found nothing funny about someone killing innocent people. SPOILER ALERT: Like the state trooper, making an innocuous traffic stop, being grabbed and shot in the head. And the man and his teenage son simply driving down the road who witness the aftermath and are murdered as a result.

Wrong place, wrong time. Sounds familiar.

On the other hand, I loved all the Bourne movies with Matt Damon. That was different. Jason Bourne was a tortured amnesiac with a conscience, anguished to discover he'd been a professional assassin in his former life. He was not a sociopath killing without remorse.

The time I really lost it in book club was when we read a bleak, twisted novel with child molestation, abuse, incest, and rape. During our book discussion, one newer member innocently said that she knew the word she was about to use was not the right one, but she couldn't think of the correct word to describe the scene where the young girl "enticed" her father.

I erupted.

"She didn't *entice* him! He molested her! Her father was a sick pervert who RAPED his daughter!"

Talk about stopping the conversation.

Not that I had any unresolved issues about the-thing-that-must-not-be-named or anything. Obviously, to everyone in the room but me, I needed to acknowledge and face those issues, but I was not quite ready to. Not yet.

I *was* ready to stop reading any book I hated or found disturbing, book club choice or not. Life is too short. There are too many books I *want* to read. Don't be forcing me to read something I don't like.

Watch something I don't like.

Eat something I don't like.

Don't be forcing me to do *any*thing. I am a grown woman and I get to say no.

Children do not have the luxury of saying no to grown-ups, particularly when those grown-ups are trusted family members. At least, when I was growing up. Good little girls in the fifties and sixties were raised to be polite and accommodating and to respect their elders. So, when a grown-up told them to do something, they usually complied. When that same grown-up told them to keep it a secret, they usually did that as well.

Thankfully, I did not have any up-close-and-personal experiences with sexual abuse as a child. Some friends and extended family members were not as fortunate.

Many families have a version of the "dirty uncle" in their family tree. Relatives roll their eyes and warn new female family members to stay away from "Uncle Harry" at holiday dinners because he's "handsy" and likes to pinch and grab.

We had our own Dirty Harry, a distant uncle by marriage who lived in a far-off state. I only saw Harry a handful of times in my life, but never felt comfortable around him. He was always teasing, flirtatious, and affectionate. Too affectionate.

A big, exuberant, grinning man, Uncle Harry would grab the girls of the family—ranging in age from five to fifteen—in bear hugs that lasted a little too long. He would also offer up effusive compliments, telling us all how pretty we were and what beauties we would be when we grew up. Often, he would pull my cousins, his "girls," over to sit on his knee, snaking his arm around their waists as he carried on a wisecracking conversation with other family members, thus effectively binding my cousins to him.

Dirty Harry also leered at and flirted with my pretty mother when we visited from out of state, pinching her as she passed by, making suggestive remarks, and telling off-color jokes I did not understand.

Mom would playfully swat his hand away, laugh, and say something like, "Now, Harry, stop that."

After our first visit when I was about eight or nine, I was worried Uncle Harry might be trying to steal my mother away from my dad. I said something to Mom about the way Harry acted. She laughed it off. "He's just teasing. He doesn't mean anything by it. Harry's all talk. If anyone ever took him up on it, he wouldn't know what to do."

Years later, after Dirty Harry had died, my cousins revealed that he had molested them growing up. Instinctively, I knew it was true. But my mom and my aunt (Harry's widow), who'd both been born in the 1930s and had a different generational mindset, had a hard time believing it.

"How come they didn't say something when he was still alive and able to defend himself?" they wondered.

Maybe because they did not feel safe?

Knew they would not be believed?

Didn't want to hurt their mother?

That's why I never told my mom about my stepfather coming on to me. Why hurt her unnecessarily? What was the point? I was in my early twenties when it happened—four years after the-thing-that-must-not-be-named.

It's not as if the dirty old man fondled me or attacked me or anything. All he did was get me alone in my apartment, leer at me with eyes full of lust, lick his ancient lips, tell me he'd had a sex dream about me, and make it clear that he'd like to make the dream a reality.

I handled it without saying a word to my mom. I fled the state. Case closed.

I wish.

A few years later when I was living back in California again, not long after my fundamentalist fiancé dumped me, Mom called me one afternoon crying and raging. She was so upset I could hardly understand her.

At home recuperating from her second mastectomy for breast cancer, initially I thought her agitation had something to do with the cancer. My heart sank. Afraid the doctor had called her with bad news, I tried to soothe Mom and figure out what she was saying. It had nothing to do with the cancer, but it was still bad news.

While my brother Todd was over visiting them, Mom mentioned that I never stayed long when my stepfather was around. She could not understand why I didn't seem to like Dick.

"Probably because he hit on her," Todd said, unthinkingly.

Mom went nuclear.

I wanted to throttle my brother for telling her. Instead, I rushed over to calm down my distraught mother. The mother still healing from a mastectomy.

When I arrived, Todd had already left for work, Mom was crying on the couch, and Dick was sitting in a nearby chair, calm and unruffled, trying to calm down his hysterical wife. My heart clenched. I hurried to my mother's side and took her hand in mine.

"It's not good for you to get so upset, Mom. Calm down. It's okay. Everything's okay."

She looked at me through red-rimmed eyes. "Did you tell Todd that Dick hit on you?"

Everything in me wanted to lie and spare her pain—the reason I had never said anything after it happened. But Mom fixed her direct gaze on me and said, "You must have misunderstood. Dick would never do that."

"Actually, he did."

I took a deep breath, not allowing myself to look in the creep's direction, yet glimpsing his gleaming head and big nose in my peripheral vision. I focused on my mother and squeezed her hand, our family signal for *I love you* that my dad, my real dad, had taught us so many years before.

"It doesn't matter. It's all in the past. Ancient history. No big deal."

Mom refused to let it go. She insisted on knowing the details. "When did this happen?" she raged, growing more and more worked up. "What did he say?"

Finally, I told her, hating the pain I was causing my mother.

Now, of all times. When I finished recounting the incident, my then-pushing-seventy stepfather said he had no memory of the occasion. He apologized if I had misunderstood something he had said and taken it the wrong way.

I looked him straight in the eye. "I didn't misunderstand anything."

Mom continued crying.

Dick adopted the dispassionate, cerebral tone he often used when explaining something to us lesser mortals. "I can't change what you believe I said years ago, or what you believe it meant, but I can apologize for any difficulty or misunderstanding I may have caused."

Sure you can, *Dick*.

My breastless, recuperating, in-pain mother looked up at me hopefully.

"No problem. Water under the bridge." I squeezed Mom's hand again and kissed her on the cheek. "Let's move on and not spend any more time talking about it. I'll go make us a nice cup of tea."

Mom and me on my wedding day.

A decade or so later, after following in my mother's breast-less steps and recovering from my own mastectomy and breast cancer treatments, I landed a job in my late thirties writing for the major daily newspaper in town, intending to be the next Woodward and Bernstein. (Watergate. Nixon. *All the President's Men.*)

Impressed? Don't be.

I wrote for the neighborhood section of the newspaper. The unwanted stepchild consigned to the boonies. And unlike Woodward and Bernstein, politics is not one of my loves. I had to cover City Council meetings, water district meetings, even cemetery district meetings. All of which I hated. I far preferred writing feature stories about real people.

Like the seventy-something woman who had been corresponding with an English pen pal for more than fifty years, whom she was finally going to meet, and the woman whose son built her a secret room in her house because she'd loved mystery stories with hidden rooms since reading Nancy Drew as a teen.

I loved writing their stories, but I also wanted to write my own.

Yet I didn't do anything tangible to pursue that writing dream until after I quit my reporting job and went to work in the marketing department of a private company for a higher salary. I continued procrastinating my writing until I had been working at the company for several months. One day I heard that the wealthy owner's wife, an accomplished chef, was writing a cookbook.

Say what? She wasn't even a writer.

Then I heard she was paying big bucks (more than my annual salary, which wasn't huge, but more than I'd ever made up to then) to a ghostwriter to turn her cookbook dreams into reality. I quit shortly thereafter and finally started writing.

Jealousy is a powerful motivator.

Finally, at thirty-nine I attended my first writers' conference with much fear and trembling. I hoped to segue from newspaper writing into magazines, although like most writers, my secret dream was to write an actual *book* someday. After reading the conference brochure and discovering there would be several book publishers present, I let my secret dream out of its long-buried hiding place, prayed, and threw together a book proposal at the last minute, not having a clue what I was doing.

The first two publishers rejected it, and I looked for a razor to slash my wrists.

I had forgotten one tiny detail. A chapter. With one chance left to submit, I grabbed the lone magazine article I had brought along and paper-clipped it to the end of my book proposal as a wannabe chapter. Then I turned it in to the manuscript submission desk and waited. Praying, stomach roiling, ready to puke.

A miracle happened.

The rock star editor from a major Christian publishing house guffawed with delight when he read my submission. *Guffawed.* Is there a sweeter word in the English language?

One year later, the week before my fortieth birthday, I received an offer for my first book from the guffawing editor, and shortly after that, an agent. I was on my way. Watch out Virginia Woolf.

Except I'm no Virginia Woolf. Joan Didion. Maya Angelou. I am not that deep. And I know and accept this about myself. My literary, more introspective friends always get mad when I say that.

"You *are* deep," they protest.

One look at the books on our respective nightstands confirms I'm right. They are reading dense theological tomes, brooding poetry, or pensive, Pulitzer Prize–winning literary fiction that I never quite understand. I am reading Trixie Belden, Agatha Christie, and Sue Grafton's alphabet mysteries.

When I was younger, I used to fight against this truth, always yearning to be deeper and more literary than I was. In my twenties, during a college creative writing class in Cleveland, the instructor often picked the same two students' work to read aloud to the class: mine and a middle-aged Black woman's. Sitting there in ill-fitting polyester, she'd had more heartache and trauma in her little finger than I'd experienced in my entire white-bread life.

Yes, there was that traumatic incident in the fraternity house, but at that point, the-thing-that-must-not-be-named still lay buried deep within my psyche. My writing pieces always made the class laugh. Hers made them weep.

Someday, I longed to make a reader weep.

17

STAINED GLASS, DOWNTON ABBEY, AND 9/11

Oh, to be in England, now that April's there.
—Robert Browning

A decade into our marriage, we returned to my beloved England on vacation. It was Michael's first visit to that sceptered isle and my first time back since I had left more than twenty years earlier. I couldn't wait to show the land of my heart to the man of my heart.

We spent a blissful week exploring the sights of Great Britain, eating fish-and-chips and Cornish pasties and having daily cream teas with yummy, proper-English scones (not the dry, elephant-sized kind found in most American coffeehouses), jam, and Devonshire cream.

Michael and I visited castles, museums, and stately manor houses. It was on that trip that we discovered ourselves drawn to English places of worship, from cathedrals to small parish churches in towns and villages. Something that had held zero interest for me when I lived there before.

The first church we visited was a marked contrast from the casual strip-mall and big-screen evangelical churches we were accustomed to in California. This beautiful, twin-towered Dorset church from the 12th century, called Wimborne Minster, was initially a nunnery and important pilgrimage site established in AD 705.

Unfortunately, my people, the Danes, destroyed the nunnery in 1013.

As we wandered slowly through the Minster, inhaling the scent of candles, wilting chrysanthemums, and old hymnals, we marveled over the ancient architecture, intricate details, and memorials to the dead. Struck by the sense of the sacred and the realization that people had been worshipping in that same place for centuries, I sat down in the nearest pew, praying as countless others had done before me and thanking God for his presence and eternal love that knows no boundaries of time or place.

The small parish churches we found in every country village stole our hearts. For Michael, it was the beauty of the stained glass. As a quilter, the piecing together of bits of color to make such a glorious picture spoke to his artist's soul. For me, the old stone churches with the scent of beeswax resonated for the same reasons I'm drawn to timeworn furniture, accessories from the past with a history, and cozy, lived-in cottages, rather than grand, overstuffed manor houses.

If *Downton Abbey* had been around then, I would have been much more at home in the Bates' humble cottage than in the Abbey (and I'd have done a much better job of hiding Lady Mary's birth-control device than her maid Anna did).

We visited a small parish church in Stow-on-the-Wold in the heaven-on-earth part of England known as the Cotswolds. There we read a lovely pastoral prayer from around 1900 that thanked God for the rolling Cotswold country, the harvest, and the animals.

The country prayer thanked God for, "the poultry and their eggs, for the dog that guards the flock or guides the blind—for the splendid horses, truest companion of man, either in patient toil or spirited adventure." It also expressed gratitude, "for the sheep, whose wool has clothed and sustained many Cotswold generations; and we humbly remember that Thine own Son, our Lord Jesus Christ, delighted to be called both the Lamb of God, and the Good Shepherd, Who loveth us forever and ever."

The date was September 11, 2001.

Since we had been sightseeing all day in the rolling green hills of the bucolic English countryside, we did not know about the attacks on the World Trade Center and the Pentagon for several hours. It was not until I stopped at a red phone booth early that evening to call my English girlfriend from back in the day, to make dinner arrangements for the next night, that I heard.

When I returned to the car, I had to tell Michael. Shocked and reeling, the terrible reality did not hit us until we got back to our B&B and our reserved English innkeeper hugged us. We began to sob.

In those early cell-phone days, our first cell phone only worked in the United States, not internationally, so we couldn't call home to check on our families. Our compassionate innkeeper kindly let us use her parlor phone, and we called home to our respective families to reassure them we were okay. (Rumors were flying that England might be attacked next, and my mom was terrified for us.)

We went up to our room and watched the horrible images on TV, images everyone else had already been watching for hours, until we could not watch anymore. Frightened and devastated, all I wanted was to return home to the States immediately to be in familiar surroundings with my family.

I *had* to get home. It was essential.

How could I stay on vacation in a land so far away when my country was falling apart and the world was in such out-of-control turmoil?

I don't do well with having control taken away. Forced to stay since there were no flights out to the U.S., we had to continue our trip and hope we would be able to return home on our scheduled flight the following week.

In this anxious and homesick state of mind, we decided the next day to visit the nearby village where I had lived with my Air Force roommate Diane more than twenty years before.

When we were stationed in England, Diane and I had rented a lovely 300-year-old, pale-pink stone cottage next to the village chapel. (The same chapel I would blast Barry Manilow at on Sunday mornings to drown out the hymns. The chapel I had never once set foot inside when I lived right next door.)

Now a good Christian, I wanted to confess my sin to the vicar and apologize for my rude, immature behavior of the past. We tried the church door, but it was locked, and no one answered when I knocked.

Then we went next door to my former home, where Michael wanted to take a picture of me standing behind the iron gate with the sign bearing the name of the cottage: Chapel Yard. I felt it might be too intrusive to the reserved Brits who likely lived there now. Michael suggested I knock on the door and ask permission, but I demurred until it occurred to me this might be my only trip back to England, and I might never get the chance again.

I knocked, and an elderly woman answered. I started to explain that I had lived there years before when stationed nearby in the Air Force—

"Laura?" she said.

It was my former landlady. The house now belonged to her daughter and family, who were away on holiday. She had only stopped by for five minutes to pick up the mail and water the plants.

Five minutes.

She invited us in, and I felt like Dorothy back home in her Kansas farmhouse murmuring, "There's no place like home... there's no place like home."

The little pink cottage, where I had lived more than two decades before, still had the same floral chintz sofa in the living room, the same matching floral curtains at the window, the same wooden table and chairs in the kitchen, and the same chintz-covered dressing table in my old upstairs bedroom. I exhaled for the first time since we had heard the horrifying news of 9/11.

There's no place like home.

Three days later, Michael and I stumbled upon a small church in the town of Woodstock that was holding a "Pray for America" service. The church was packed, but people squeezed in and made room for us at a pew up front. It was obvious we were Americans by our jeans, backpacks, and flat accents amongst all the well-dressed Brits in their church best and posh accents.

We sang the hymn "Immortal, Invisible, God Only Wise," and then there was a reading from Isaiah.

The Lord...hath sent me to bind up the brokenhearted...to comfort all that mourn...to give unto them beauty for ashes, the oil of joy for mourning, the garment of praise for the spirit of heaviness...And they shall build the old wastes, they shall raise up the former desolations, and they shall repair the waste cities...

I wept.

After the reading, we all said Psalm 46 together.

God is our refuge and strength,
A very present help in trouble.

Therefore we will not fear, though the earth should change,
though the mountains shake in the heart of the sea;
   . . . God is in the midst of the city; it shall not be moved;
   God will help it when the morning dawns. . .

Saying the same words aloud together unified us all as we stood shoulder-to-shoulder in that little church weeping. During the three minutes of silence that fell across England and the rest of Europe, as the continent joined the United States in its National Day of Prayer and Remembrance, the message we received was, "We must not hate."

Our country just suffered a horrifying, unprovoked attack where thousands of innocent people lost their lives because of fanatic extremists, and you do not want us to hate, God?

Pieces of Scripture leached through my grief: *Do not repay anyone evil for evil...live at peace with everyone. Do not take revenge...Do not be overcome by evil, but overcome evil with good.*

We sang "The Battle Hymn of the Republic," and as our mouths formed the words to the final verse printed in the program, the tears ran unchecked down our faces and the faces of those around us.

Mine eyes have seen the glory
   Of the coming of the Lord;
   It is flowing through the cities
   And the waste will be restored;
   By the leading of the Spirit
   And their trusting in His Word
   His army marches on...

SITTING AT THE KIDS' TABLE

The soul is healed by being with children.
—English Proverb

In my late forties, I fell in love with little kids. Who knew? I don't know whether it was my delayed maternal instinct finally kicking in, or that last rush of hormones before I went into early menopause. But suddenly, everywhere I went I became a mass of mushy, gushing gooiness every time I saw children. Especially toddlers. My heart would melt into a puddle of pure joy and love for the whole world at the sight of their sweet smiling faces, wispy fine hair, and chubby little legs propelling them forward.

Hanging out with little kids became one of my favorite pastimes. At holiday meals with our large extended family, I would always make the supreme sacrifice of offering to sit at the kids' table.

"No, you take a break and sit with the grown-ups," I would say to the frazzled young moms who were grateful for a little adult conversation. "I've got this."

I would sit with my favorite little ones, cut their meat, and encourage them to eat at least two more bites of their meal, as required by their mom and dad, so we could then go play in the other room. There I would spin stories like Scheherazade for my great-nieces and nephews. Fantastical tales of pirates, dragons, superheroes, and princesses (constantly, princesses).

My great-nieces Lexi and Emily, whom I adored, always wanted stories about beautiful princesses and their sparkly clothes and jewels. I made sure the princesses were all strong and adventurous with magical powers, explaining to the adorable duo that the greatest power any princess possessed was kindness.

"But did she also have a pretty pink crown with lots of jewels?"

Other times, I'd flop my now fifty-something body on the floor with the kids and play trains, Candy Land, and the memory game where we'd have to match playing cards, all the while marveling aloud at their amazing prowess.

Four-year-old Emily would look at me sympathetically and say, "You're not very good at remembering, are you?"

"Nope. I'm old. That's what happens when you get old." (I was around fifty-two at this point.)

"That's okay, I'll help you," she would say, patting my hand.

Emily's older sister, Lexi, gushed love like a volcano. Whenever her mom pulled up in front of our house and was busy getting Emily out of her car seat, Lexi opened her passenger door onto the grass, jumped out, and barreled across the front yard to me yelling, "Aunt Lala!" as she flung herself into my arms.

Lexi was good at flinging.

Like the year at our extended family Christmas brunch, when she flung her little arms around the legs of an older male cousin she'd just met, who was going to Disneyland the following week. Lexi clung to her cousin's calves, looked up at him beseechingly, and said, "I'll help."

I became a surrogate grandma to Lexi and Emily. Those little girls stole my heart. So much so that we returned to church to see them every Sunday.

There had also been the guilt factor about not going to church. Jewish mothers have nothing on backslidden born-agains. But community is important, so we decided to start attending Lexi and Emily's church. Even though it was big and Baptist.

This big Baptist church had the standard worship and praise band with the customary praise songs on the ubiquitous large screens, so we could all sing and clap along. There was a lot of clapping. One Sunday the pastor said, "Let's give the Lord a hand!" The church exploded in applause. That applause repeated week after week as they continued to clap for Jesus.

My wrist beneath my WWJD bracelet began to itch.

I would stop scratching whenever I hung out with Lexi and Emily. After church, we would go out to breakfast with their family, which the girls and I rushed through so we could get to the good stuff. After finishing their croissants and asking to be excused, Lexi and Emily would tug on my arm. "C'mon, Aunt Lala, let's go outside and play." The girls grabbed my hands and made a beeline to the courtyard while Michael stayed inside talking to the adults.

"You can't catch me, Lala," said Lexi, giggling, as she ran around the potted tree in the courtyard, her little sister hard on her heels.

"Yeah, you can't catch us," Emily echoed.

"Oh yes, I can," I said in a mock growl, advancing upon them. "I'm going to get you!"

They shrieked and giggled and ran in circles around the tree even faster, until they got dizzy, and we all collapsed on a bench together. Then it was princess story time. Lexi and Emily were besotted with the Disney princesses, especially Belle and Ariel, so I always had to knit them into my fractured fairytales. Sometimes the girls would protest that I got the story wrong, but I'd quell their objections by weaving them into my tale and making Lexi and Emily the stars of the story instead, leaving Belle in the dust and Ariel in the moat.

I looked forward to my special Sunday time with my surrogate granddaughters each week. Being with them gave me the kid-fix I craved.

Then our precious six-year-old Lexi died.

Two months before, when Michael and I were out Christmas shopping, I had a sudden and urgent compulsion to buy Lexi and Emily Christmas dresses. I had never done so before. That was a privilege usually afforded their biological grandmothers.

"I know I'm only their surrogate grandma, and I don't want to step on either grandmother's toes," I told Michael. "But I really, really want to buy them both a pretty dress for the holidays this year. It's important to me. I don't know why, but it is."

Since I did not want to run the risk of buying them a duplicate dress one of the other grandmas might have already gotten them, we went to a nearby department store that I knew neither grandmother frequented. I sifted through rack after rack of velvet and sequins until finally I found the perfect dress for four-year-old Emily: a rich red taffeta with a white Peter Pan collar, three white bows across the bodice, and a full skirt with a crackly petticoat underneath.

Lexi's dress was more difficult to find since she was older and taller. As the sizes increased, so did the sleaze factor. *What is with all the tight, black Vegas showgirl stuff?* At last, at the back of the very last rack, I found a lone size-six red velvet, long-sleeved dress with white mock-fur cuffs and collar that reminded me of the dresses Rosemary Clooney and Vera Ellen wore at the end of *White Christmas*, my favorite holiday movie. A dainty white satin bow with a small, red, sparkly flower in the center and a trailing ribbon pinned to the fluffy fur collar added the perfect final touch.

I couldn't wait to take the dresses over to the girls.

"You want to give them to them now?" Michael asked. "Christmas is still three weeks away."

"I know, but this is a *pre*-Christmas gift, and I can't wait to see their faces."

One of the best moments of my life.

Lexi's and Emily's eyes lit up like their Christmas tree when they opened their dress boxes. Lexi rubbed the fluffy fur collar against her cheek. "Ooh, Mommy, can we put them on now?"

"Sure. That way we can all see them." Jennie left to help her daughters change.

Five minutes later, the girls raced back into the living room. Forget Rosemary Clooney and Vera Ellen. Lexi and her little sister stole their White Christmas crown that day.

I keep a framed picture of Lexi and Emily in those red Christmas dresses on a shelf in our dining room corner cupboard where I can see it every day.

Emily is looking shyly at something beyond the camera, her hands clasped in front of her, but Lexi is gazing straight at me, a slight smile on her lips, her long, honey-colored hair curling softly against her white fur collar, her right arm hugging the neck of her baby sister.

Lexi died two months later.

We all thought it was from a bad case of the flu going around, but later learned it was Reye's syndrome, a rare but deadly disease which usually follows a viral infection and attacks without warning.

Jennie and Jason, Lexi's parents, had taken their sick young daughter to the hospital while I was at work. Michael's sister Sheri—Jennie's mom and Lexi's grandmother—called me at my office.

"They had to resuscitate Lexi," Sheri said.

"What?!" I yelled. I called Michael, and together we raced to the hospital. When we arrived, we saw Lexi in an ICU bed surrounded by her parents, both grandmothers, a doctor, and a couple nurses.

As we approached, I gave Lexi, whose head was turned my way, an encouraging yet tremulous smile as I tried to hold the tears at bay so as not to frighten her.

The medical staff moved away from the bed, talking in low voices. Jason, Lexi's father, kissed his daughter on the forehead while one grandmother stroked Lexi's hair and the other grandmother gently stroked her foot. Jennie, who was holding her firstborn daughter's hand and murmuring to her, beckoned me forward.

"I love you, Lexi," I said, lightly rubbing her leg. But she was lethargic and listless and did not respond.

Loving family hands continued to gently touch and make contact with our beloved little girl. More relatives arrived, including Jennie's twin sister Kari, Lexi's favorite and much-adored Aunt "Kitty."

The ICU grew crowded, and a nurse encouraged some of us to wait in the waiting room, particularly since Lexi had stabilized. Thanking God and releasing a huge sigh of relief, Michael and I retreated down the hall to give immediate family room with sweet Lexi.

Since Jennie, Jason, Sheri, and other family members had been at the hospital for hours without sustenance, Michael left to make a food run. When he returned to the waiting room, we began pulling fast-food tacos out of the bag. All at once, one of the nurses rushed in.

"You'd better come," she said urgently. "It's not looking good."

My heart ripped from my chest as we raced back to the ICU. As we drew near, we heard both Jennie's and Sheri's anguished wails.

"No!"

One of the worst moments of my life.

Lexi's death left us with a bleeding, gaping hole where our hearts used to be.

After the unfathomable, soul-crushing loss of this beautiful child, who was so full of life and laughter, we heard every trite saying imaginable. Actually, it was unimaginable. It was impossible to imagine the ridiculously stupid and thoughtless things that came out of the mouths of people.

Especially at church.

"She's in a better place."

No, her place is with her parents and younger sister Emily who all adore her and are lost without her.

"God needed a new angel."

Well then, let him make one.

"What a glorious homegoing this was!"

Are you f—ing kidding me? There is nothing glorious about an innocent, six-year-old child being taken away without warning from the family who loves her.

Six. Years. Old.

"Maybe the Lord took her home to bring her daddy to Christ."

That was the final nail in the church coffin.

19

FAMILY AND OTHER F-WORDS

*The friend who can be silent with us in a moment of despair or
confusion, who can stay with us in an hour of grief and bereavement,
who can tolerate not knowing...not healing, not curing...
that is a friend who cares.*
—Henri M. Nouwen

W e don't have children, but we're close to our
nieces and nephews. Michael's twin nieces,
Jennie and Kari, have been like daughters to him
since the day they were born. Michael drove his older sister
Sheri to the hospital when she went into labor and cradled
those twin baby girls in his arms five minutes after they were
born. They hold a special place in his heart.

Jennie and Kari look upon Michael (or as they've called him
since childhood, *Meeka-Mike*, since they couldn't pronounce
"Uncle") as a second father.

When Lexi died that awful day in the ICU, Michael saw his
niece Jennie, whom he loves like a daughter, weeping over the
daughter she had just lost. It cut him to the core.

Some cuts are deeper still.

After Lexi died, her parents and grandparents were so shattered they could barely function. Michael and I and other extended family members stepped up and handled many of the myriad heartbreaking details that follow an unexpected death. That's what you do. Whatever you can to provide some small measure of help and comfort in the face of such a tragic, heartrending loss. Someone must be strong and deal with the practical, necessary particulars, and Michael and I were good at that. We became the go-to couple in times of family crises.

A couple weeks after Lexi's memorial service, we returned to our Wednesday night small group of disaffected evangelicals that met in the home of a young former pastor named Keith and his wife, Char. That night when we arrived, Char, who has two sons about the same age as Lexi and Emily, hugged me, tears flooding her face.

"I'm so sorry."

That did it. I began to sob and sob. Then I began to rant through my sobs.

"I'm so sick of frickin' evangelical Christians and their stupid trite platitudes and Bible verses. They need to shut the fuck up! A six-year-old girl died. She DIED! Her family is devastated. No parent should have to outlive their child. It's not right."

Snot dripped from my running nose, and I wiped it away with the back of my hand. "And if one more person says, 'She's in a better place,' I'll shove that better place up their fucking fundamentalist ass!"

Michael stared at me. He had never heard words like that come from my mouth.

Neither had I.

As the oldest, most etiquette-conscious member of the Wednesday night group, and one who hates conflict and yelling, courtesy of my mother, I don't normally swear. Especially not f-bombs.

But that night, all bets were off. I raged and ranted, then raged and ranted some more. Char poured me a glass of sangria and handed it to me like a communion cup. I gulped down the fruity wine between sobs, slurping up the strawberries.

She poured me another glass. I drained that too.

Then I curled up on the couch and fell asleep.

More and more, I could relate to Gandhi when he said, "I like your Christ; I do not like your Christians."

In the late eighties, when I was a single, new evangelical and thought I had all the answers, I worked briefly at an advertising agency, where the graphic designer was a kind, funny gay man who had grown up in the Bible belt and could not tell his fundamentalist Christian parents he was gay, or they would disown him. He led a secret life in California they knew nothing about, and when he went back home to visit, or they came out to visit him, he carefully hid that secret life from them.

The conflict with his true self and his upbringing caused him great anguish. To cope with that anguish, my coworker drank. Sometimes when he drank, we would have discussions on the Bible, purity, and homosexuality.

"Why is it wrong?" he would ask. "It's who I am, and God made me."

"Sin is sin," I would reply self-righteously from my celibate ivory tower. "And sex outside of marriage is a sin." Then I would console him by saying, "We're in the same boat. Since I'm not married, I'm not allowed to have sex either; it would be the same kind of sin."

"The difference is you have the chance of getting married and having sex someday," he'd say, taking another swig from the bottle. "I don't."

I did not know how to respond to that, so I simply kept parroting what I had learned in church: sexual purity was everything.

Now, I would ask my friend's forgiveness for my smug righteousness and admit I don't have all the answers. I don't know all the answers. What I do know is that Jesus said to love your neighbor as you love yourself, and in the love chapter in Corinthians so often quoted at weddings, it ends, *And now abide faith, hope, love, these three; but the greatest of these is love.*

In my early fundie days, I adopted the prevailing, old-school Christian attitude that feminism was a bad thing. It went against the natural, Biblical roles established for men and women where men were the leaders. And women? The submissive followers. I even wrote a chapter called "Submission Impossible" in my first Christian humor book, *Dated Jekyll, Married Hyde.* (Thankfully now out of print.)

A few months after my fundamentalist fiancé dumped me, I had dinner with a male friend from my former church. The church I had to leave since it was too associated with my ex. The one where everyone told me God had a better plan for me. Halfway through the meal, my male friend, whom I knew had a little crush on me and who apparently thought the dinner was a date, said, "I don't think I'll be able to go out with you. I think you'll have a hard time being submissive."

I choked on my steak. *Ya think?*

Yet I still recall my horror during my early born-again days when a young college friend from the campus Christian group used the f-word to describe Jesus. Sacrilege. How dare he call Jesus a feminist.

This from the girl who read *Ms.* magazine in high school, challenged the boys to a game of touch football, and flew off into that wild blue yonder with Uncle Sam's Air Force. I had really come a long way, baby.

In time, I came out of my fundie fog and realized Jesus *was* a feminist. Jesus was pro-woman. He treated women equally to men and involved them in his ministry. Happily, I also married a man who believed in equality. A strong, confident man secure in his masculinity, who told me he did not want a doormat for a wife.

And he even cooks and sews.

Michael and me during chemo days.

20

PUCCINI AND PEW WORKOUTS

I'm an Episcopal, which is Catholic Lite.
It's like same religion, half the guilt.
—Robin Williams

While stationed in England in the late 1970s, most weekends my Air Force gal pals and I used to go dancing at a gay bar in Oxford. Daring stuff for a straight good girl like me. The DJ played the best music in town, and you did not need a guy to dance.

Six or seven of us would put on our best threads and cram into my roommate's Mini for the drive to Oxford. (I usually wore a sexy little black dress or slinky harem pants, a glittery tube top, and stiletto heels.) We never arrived before ten o'clock and danced the night away to such disco favorites as "YMCA," "I Will Survive," and the ubiquitous "Dancing Queen," which usually ended the night and brought every gay man in the room onto the dance floor.

The great thing about the too-crowded space was that it disguised my pathetic dance moves. I am a terrible dancer. I have enthusiasm, but no skill or natural ability.

Or as one of my journalism classmates said when I, a life-long member of the grammar police, primly corrected her spelling and told her there was no "u" in rhythm: "No, there's no YOU in rhythm."

Recognizing my limitations and unwilling to inflict that painful torture on the world's eyeballs, I stopped dancing years ago. Except for the rare slow dance, a limited shuffle-step-glide in a two-foot circle, at the occasional wedding with Michael, who's also dance-impaired. Then a few years ago I was at a friend's wedding reception, when a group of us were sitting watching the people on the dance floor, and "Dancing Queen" started filtering through the speakers.

"I love this song!" I said, twitching my shoulders and tapping my foot.

My gay friend Shane, who loves to dance and does so coolly and effortlessly, grabbed my hand and pulled me to the dance floor. Shane had the smoothest moves on the floor. I looked like a jerky puppet doing "the white man's overbite," as Billy Crystal says.

In a 2007 study done by The Barna Group, when young people in America aged 16-29 were asked what words best described Christianity, the top response was "anti-homosexual." Young people have been leaving the church in droves due to the intolerance, bigotry, uncaring attitudes, and hostility of angry right-wing evangelicals. Particularly toward gays.

Not just young people.

When we walked away from the evangelical church in our early fifties, we didn't know if we would ever return to houses of worship again. With so much ugliness in the world—wars, rumors of wars, school shootings, hatred of people who love differently than we do—my soul longed for beauty and peace. Sadly, I could not find that in church anymore.

Instead, we stayed home on Sundays and listened to Puccini. Nothing like a little Puccini in the morning to feed the soul. I played "O Mio Babbino Caro" repeatedly, closing my eyes at the sheer gorgeousness of this aria that moves me to the very core of my being and transports me to another plane. It is my go-to piece of music when life is hard, people are mean, or family is driving me crazy.

Then I basked in the beauty of "Gabriel's Oboe," the haunting theme from the '80s movie *The Mission* that reminds me to be still and know that God is with me. As I let the music absorb into my soul, I drink in the beauty made by the verdant canopy of trees that rings our backyard. As I sat in my favorite chair, sipping a cup of PG Tips with our American Eskimo, Gracie, sprawled on the warm grass at my feet, and through eyes slitted against the sun, I watch the green leaves of the camphor tree brush against the claret-colored plum cherry leaves, dancing shadows on the ground.

Anne Frank said the best remedy for those who are afraid, lonely, or unhappy is to go outside, somewhere where they can be quiet, alone with the heavens, nature, and God, because only then does one feel that all is as it should be.

Outside in the stillness, punctuated only by birdsong and a breeze rustling the trees, my soul felt that all was as it should be.

During our retreat from church, we dreamed of England. Had circumstances and budget allowed, we'd have retreated to the bucolic English countryside, breathed in all that pastoral serenity, and taken refuge in the small village churches.

Michael has a great book called *England's Thousand Best Churches*, which we used as our guide on our second trip to England.

On that trip, two years after 9/11, I, too, fell in love with stained glass after visiting a 15th century Cotswold church called St. Mary's in the village of Fairford.

St. Mary's contains England's only complete set of medieval narrative stained glass. That narrative glass encompassed twenty-eight vibrant, multicolored windows that used to teach the Christian faith by pictures for almost 500 years. The first window depicts the serpent offering the fruit to Eve in the Garden of Eden, while successive windows contain Biblical scenes, including Christ's birth, crucifixion, and resurrection.

The centerpiece technicolor window of The Last Judgment mesmerized me with its terrible beauty. Christ sits enthroned on a blue and amber rainbow, the earth his footstool. Mary kneels on his left, John the Baptist on his right, and martyrs and angels encircle him in a rich blood red that came alive in vivid color when the sun shone through the glass. I could not take my eyes off Jesus and the blood red surrounding him.

In that little country church so far from home, he filled me with his presence in a way I had never known in the countless megachurches. At those megachurches, and most every other evangelical church I have attended, I always heard that the "High Church" Protestant denominations were spiritually "dead" and filled with empty, meaningless ritual. Episcopalians and the like were dubbed "the frozen chosen."

They said the church in England was dead too.

It did not feel dead to me when I attended Evensong, gazed on the glorious stained glass, or sang hymns in unison with my Christian brothers and sisters after that terrible day on 9/11. It felt rich. Reverent. And holy. These sacred surroundings and beautiful tributes of praise and glory to God spoke to my soul.

Keats said, "beauty is truth, truth beauty." What a glorious manifestation of beauty and truth bound together.

One Palm Sunday, more than two years after we walked away from church, we hesitantly decided to visit a neighborhood

Episcopal church. Michael had heard about the church from an actor friend whose wife was the rector.

I loved the sound of that. Both the word rector, which was so very English to my Anglophile ears, and that the church had a woman pastor.

Women aren't allowed to preach in church. For years, I had that patriarchal fundamentalist rule drummed into my good-Christian-girl head. Women cannot lead men. They can teach Bible studies but not have *authority* over men, which meant no women preaching from the pulpit. That always bugged the dormant feminist in me, but for years I squelched that side of myself to fit in.

Now that I had left those churches, *she* was awakening again.

One thing for sure, these Episcopalians were far from the frozen chosen. They were all active participants in the service. One of the most reverent church services I have ever attended. The liturgy, which many evangelicals say is boring and repetitive, was a thing of beauty.

But there was a lot of standing up, sitting down, kneeling, and standing up and sitting down again. Nothing like a little pew aerobics on a Sunday morning to wake you up.

Much of the service was unfamiliar to me, including the hymns and *The Book of Common Prayer*, but I recognized and have always loved the doxology:

Praise God from whom all blessings flow;
Praise Him, all creatures here below;
Praise Him above, ye heavenly host;
Praise Father, Son, and Holy Ghost. Amen.

Before Communion, or as they called it, the Eucharist, a white-haired priest with an earring, serving as what I thought was a cantor, but the bulletin called a celebrant, sang:

Celebrant: The-uh Lord be-e wi-ith you.
People: An-and also with you.
Celebrant: Li-i-ift u-u-up your hear-arts.
People: We li-i-ift them to-o-o the Lo-ord.
Celebrant: Let us give thay-an-anks to the Lo-ord our Ga-od.
People: It is ri-i-ight to give him thay-anks and pra-aise.

It reminded me of a Jewish synagogue or Catholic church. Later, I learned the Episcopal Church is called "Catholic-lite," which explained why people were making the sign of the cross. They showed other signs of respect too. As each person left their pew and stepped into the center aisle on their way to receive Communion, they would execute a slight bow or curtsy to the altar, the way people do when presented to royalty. When the Gospel was raised high and carried down that same aisle, heads bowed.

Call me old-fashioned, but the respect and reverence in that church really spoke to my Emily Post heart. So did the love, kindness, acceptance, inclusiveness, and humility I observed. These days, for me, it is all about kindness and love.

Jesus said, *Just as I have loved you, you are to love one another.*

During the peace-be-with-you exchange among the congregants, I observed a couple eighty-something-looking parishioners talking to a beaming, middle-aged gay man and saw them embrace him in a warm hug.

We were so coming back.

We were eager to return to the Episcopal church. Wait, eager to return to *church*? Not something that had been part of our vocabulary for a few years. Clearly, this little church had something. The Sunday after Easter—which we had to miss due to family commitments—our non-churchy butts were back in those Episcopal pews. They fit us well. The Episcopal Church is an offshoot of the Church of England.

No wonder our Anglophile hearts felt at home there.

In advance of our return, I had cruised the church website and found the rector's notes to the congregation from her recent sabbatical to England. I felt an instant connection. She, too, was an Anglophile who had grown up reading English novels and loved English china and "all things BBC." My kind of woman, er...rector. Not only that, but she had also visited and fallen in love with Chipping Camden, one of our favorite Cotswold towns.

It was a sign.

The Episcopal Church was beautiful and mysterious. An entirely new world to me, complete with colorful clergy clothing. I learned that Episcopalians follow a three-legged stool approach: scripture, tradition, and reason—needing all three to keep balance.

As we recited the Nicene Creed together, I was happy to discover we believed the same important basics. Something about saying the same words aloud together, as we did in the English church after 9/11, unifies us as we stand shoulder-to-shoulder in the sanctuary. Some claim that it is rote and meaningless recitation.

Not to me.

As a writer and lover of words, when I say the poetic, lyrical words of the liturgy, it helps me affirm what I believe, who God is, and who I am in God. When I say those words each week, I mean them.

Pastor Mary, the rector, was smart, soft-spoken, and small in stature. She radiated strength, intelligence, and kindness. When she preached, Pastor Mary spoke of the grace and love of

God. We were to discover that it was a recurring theme amongst all the clergy.

"We are to love as God loves, forgive as God forgives, have compassion as God has compassion," proclaimed Father George, the white-haired seventy-something priest with the earring. "In short, love the Lord our God with all of our hearts, minds, souls, and bodies, and love our neighbors as ourselves. This is our constant. God's love never changes."

One Sunday, Pastor Mary announced they would be holding a Blessing of the Animals service in honor of St. Francis, where parishioners could bring their beloved pets and have them blessed. Michael and I exchanged happy looks when we heard the announcement. That was our favorite *Vicar of Dibley* episode. (The most iconic episode in Britcom history. Geraldine, the vicar, played by the hilarius Dawn French, blessed a variety of dogs, cats, cows, horses, pigs, sheep, rabbits, ducks, birds, a snake, and one stuffed Teddy bear.)

We had been attending the church for a few months when we took part in its annual craft fair. During the preparation, things got a little chaotic, and I overheard one of the frazzled organizers, a woman who looked to be in her early seventies, say, "This has gone wrong, and that has gone wrong, and I'm out of vodka."

Later, another longtime church member, a fun, welcoming woman who looked to be in her late fifties—I later found out was close to seventy—upon hearing the story of my ex-fundie fiancé who insisted that his wife sew, said, "Oh, fuck no."

I knew I'd found my people.

Each week at church, our rector Reverend Mary, the "new" rector who succeeded Pastor Mary upon her retirement (it is not a requirement for our rectors to be female or named

Mary), ends the service with this blessing adapted from the Swiss poet and philosopher Henri Frederic Amiel:

Life is short and we do not have much time to gladden the hearts of those who travel the way with us. So be quick to love, and make haste to be kind. And may the Divine Mystery, who is beyond our ability to know, but who made us, and who loves us, and who travels the way with us, Bless you and Keep you in peace. Amen.

21

MAKE A JOYFUL NOISE

*Beautiful music is the art of the prophets that can calm
the agitations of the soul; it is one of the most magnificent
and delightful presents God has given us.*
—Martin Luther

One of the things I love about our Episcopal church is the choir. And I'm not saying that because I'm in the choir. I loved it even before I joined.

They sang such gorgeous, classical music: Handel, Haydn, Mendelssohn, Mozart, Bach. In addition to familiar classic composers, the choir also sang many pieces I had never heard before, sometimes in French or Latin. It may not be a big deal to some, but to a woman who spent her entire evangelical church life raising her hands and singing contemporary praise songs with simple repetitive choruses that all began to sound alike after a while, I appreciated the beauty and complexity of this glorious liturgical music.

To be able to sing that beauty is a privilege. When I sing that sacred music, composed to exalt and honor God, it brings me closer to him and I can feel his majesty. His holiness. In

Thomas Carlyle's words: "Music is well said to be the speech of angels."

I never expected to be singing hymns. I'm not a classically trained musician, but I love to sing and I especially love hearing the four-part harmony. Believe it or not, I am a first soprano. I am so rockin' that sopranos section. (Not really, but a girl can dream.) I plan to sing first soprano as long as I can, since they usually sing the melody and I don't have a clue how to sing harmony. The altos get stuck with that.

I'll let you in on a little secret, but don't tell my choir director: I can't read music. I know when notes go up or down and when I'm supposed to hold a note, but that's about it. Mostly I just fake it. I watch our director vigilantly, listen carefully to what the sopranos next to me sing, and copy them. When I'm unfamiliar with the song we're rehearsing (often), I sing quietly so no one will figure me out for the fraud I am. But when it's a song I know, like "It Is Well with My Soul," I let it go like Idina Menzel.

I sit next to my friend Kate, who is a strong soprano with a gorgeous voice. Next to her is Paula, another strong soprano with a beautiful voice. The first time I heard them sing the duet of "Pie Jesu," I got chills. (I have already booked them to sing that at my funeral. It's good to be prepared.)

There are about thirty people in our choir with a fifty-year age span among us, which includes a couple octogenarians and one soprano in her nineties, who still has a killer voice. Most of those choir members really know their stuff. Many have studied music and come from a musical background. When the real musicians talk about the piece we are rehearsing, it is a foreign language to me, just as tongues were in the evangelical church. The diminuendo after the glissando is like a sforzando.

Say what? Not my forte. I am a seat-of-the-pants singer. Michael just read this over my shoulder and informed me "forte" is a musical term. Guess it's seeping into my consciousness after all.

Sometimes during our weekly rehearsal, a choir member will ask the director, "Isn't that a G?" They might as well be saying, "Isn't that a W?" for all the meaning it holds for me. And do not even get me started on the counting: 4/4 time, 2/4 time, 6/8 time. Math has never been my friend. Not as a child. Not as an adult. Thanks to my right brain, nontechnical nature. Math gives me a headache. I do not want to do arithmetic; I just want to sing.

I wing it and it works.

Our classically trained choir director Connie demands excellence and brings out the best in us. Sometimes she has more faith in our abilities than we do. She gives us brand-new music some of us have never seen. Which we then must sight-read. In Latin. We're trying to figure out how to pronounce the words as well as what notes to sing while trying to watch Connie for the cutoffs.

Good thing we're ambidextrous.

One of the highlights of the church year is Christmas, or as Episcopalians and other high church denominations call the entire season, Advent. (Wait...that's not quite right. I sent this chapter to Connie—which means I'm now busted on the whole I-can't-read-music secret—to ensure its accuracy.) She explained that Advent is the beginning of the liturgical church year and is comprised of the four Sundays preceding Christmas. Christmas starts Christmas Day and is twelve days long.

Ah. Now that "On the first day of Christmas, my true love gave to me..." song finally makes sense.

The choral focal point during the holiday season is a service called Lessons and Carols, usually held the last Sunday before Christmas. The entire service is comprised of readings (lessons) and special music (carols). No sermon necessary. I'd never sung in so many different languages before. French. Latin. German. Middle English.

I have loved French ever since ninth-grade French class. It is such a beautiful, romantic language, so getting to sing in French was a special treat and brought back memories of a much-loved, romantic trip to Paris with Michael. I had no firsthand experience with Latin, but when we sang "Magnificat," the sheer beauty and history of that ancient language blew me away.

Occasionally, before rehearsal begins, our director will share a devotion with the choir, which she writes centered on a certain hymn, and then has us sing the hymn together. One of those devotions focused on the 17th century hymn "Praise to God," or as it is better known: "Praise to the Lord, the Almighty, the King of Creation." When she concluded the devotion, Connie said, "Music is to lift the masses up, for that's where heaven is."

Each week, when we sing, I am lifted up.

Our choir is a family. We sing together, pray together, play together, and support one another in good times and bad. When one of our beloved members, Donald, passed away unexpectedly a few years ago while out jogging, the choir surrounded his long-time, much-loved, and devastated partner David with Christ's love and compassion. David later told us that many of their LGBTQ friends remarked upon the overwhelming kindness, acceptance, and love our church showed them at Donald's memorial service.

So different from the reception they were accustomed to from most churches.

That is what keeps us at our neighborhood Episcopal church. That and our weekly celebration of the Eucharist. Communion. The Lord's Supper. Everyone is welcome at the table, no matter their age, background, belief system, race, gender, sexual orientation, or politics. The rich. The poor. The lonely. The popular. The young. The old. The infirm. The outcasts. The misfits. The marginalized. . .

All are hungry and all may come and partake of the bread and wine. In that moment when they do, something beautiful and mysterious happens. We are all in communion with God and each other.

We are all part of the family of God.

22

HELL AND FAREWELL

Neurotics build castles in the air; psychotics live in them.
My mother cleans them.
—Rita Rudner

During my breast cancer battle in my mid-thirties, my cancer survivor mom was right by my side. My mother and I had developed a much closer relationship when I became a grown-up. Especially once I realized that being a young waitress mom in her twenties with four kids under the age of ten and always living on the financial edge must have taken its toll.

As adults, Mom and I would do girly things together, like go to lunch, have tea, even shop. She enjoyed shopping more than me. That happens when you're size six and can find cute clothes. I haven't seen size six since the womb.

Back in my high school days, Mom had always been the biggest cheerleader of my writing. Since I became a published author, she was even more so. She would sit front and center at my book signings, send dozens of copies to her friends and relatives, and tell strangers and grocery store clerks that her daughter was an AUTHOR.

It was a little embarrassing. But not too much.

In 2000, the month before my forty-fourth birthday, when my publisher sent me on a six-city book tour for *Thanks for the Mammogram!*, Michael accompanied me. We also took Mom along on the New York and Chicago legs of the tour, so she could see the Big Apple and visit family back in Wisconsin.

Money was tight, so in New York, the three of us squeezed into the same hotel room with two queen-size beds, provided by my publisher. Not exactly the romantic rendezvous my husband had hoped for our first time together in the city that never sleeps.

I promised Michael we'd return. Someday.

Our first night, we dropped our bags in the hotel room and headed for Times Square and Broadway. Yellow cabs honked, lights flashed, and waves of people washed against us like a tsunami.

On Broadway at Les Miz. Bliss.

"Ooh, look, there's *CATS*. *Annie Get Your Gun*. *Les Miz*. Tomorrow night we're going to *Les Miz*!"

I was able to help make one of my mother's lifelong dreams come true by taking her to a Broadway play. My publicist friend Twila, who accompanied us, snapped a picture of Mom, Michael, and me beaming in front of the *Les Misérables* marquee.

The following night I had a cancer-speaking gig at Gilda's Club—named for comedian Gilda Radner, who died of ovarian cancer in her early forties. Mom planned to go along and sit front and center as she usually does at my talks. Instead, Michael told her he was taking her on a date.

She still sat front and center, but at the Metropolitan Opera, twenty feet from her favorite singer, Placido Domingo.

We are given moments like these to take out and hold in our hands when the bad times come. And the bad times always come. Sometimes they are so bad you don't think you can hang on. That is when your friends, family, and church come alongside you, grab your hand, and pull you up from the ledge.

Less than a decade after our New York trip, Mom began to decline.

Lung cancer. Emphysema. A broken hip. COPD (Chronic Obstructive Pulmonary Disease). Fibromyalgia. Pneumonia. Severe osteoporosis that compacted her normal five-foot-four-inch frame down to four-foot-eleven. Mom spent her seventy-third birthday in hospice, weighing sixty-four pounds and days away from death.

Two months later, my strong-willed mother graduated from hospice, thanks to the amazing care of a Romanian woman named Didi. Nearly a year later, thanks to Didi's healthy cooking at the board-and-care home, Mom topped the scales at 100.

Mom was better for a couple years but still lived in constant pain, taking more medications than I inhaled chocolate. She moved slowly, had to use a walker to get around, and used oxygen at night. Mom stopped cooking, driving, and balancing her checkbook because she was starting to get forgetful. She made Michael her financial power of attorney and me her medical power of attorney.

By this time, my mother had moved into an assisted-living home near us, where they could monitor her myriad meds and provide daily meals. Michael and I had tried having Mom live with us, but with both of us working full-time, it just didn't work. (There was also that little thing about having two high-maintenance, take-charge, Type A women living in tight quarters together. Michael nearly moved out to a hotel during that period.)

It was difficult for Mom to downsize, but she had the best decorated room in the assisted living community, complete with her beloved cherry wood lingerie chest, computer (she couldn't live without Slingo and email), favorite family photos, and delicate china teacups. The staff, with her permission, always showed prospective tenants Mom's room as an example of how they could make their own rooms into home sweet home.

At this new home, my mother soon earned the name "the cookie queen" for dispensing cookies to her new friends and staff. It was my job and my sister's to keep Mom supplied in cookies, Danish, peppermints, wet wipes, and Depends. The last one was the hardest thing for me to buy my classy, etiquette-conscious mother who had always been such a lady and taken such pride in her appearance.

One spring day, one of the aides at the home called to tell me Mom had fallen, and the ambulance was taking her to the hospital. My heart clenched. The last time she had fallen, Mom had broken her hip. This time, thankfully, the medics said nothing was broken, but she was pale and clammy and needed to be checked out.

We met them at the ER and entered six weeks of hell.

After spending all day and night at the hospital while they poked and prodded my poor mother and ran a bunch of tests, Mom sent me home so she could sleep. I walked in my front door a few minutes after ten and crashed. Just over an hour later the on-call hospital surgeon called me.

"Your mother has an intestinal blockage, and as her power of attorney, I need your consent to do surgery immediately." The surgeon then proceeded to rattle off a host of dire things that could happen during surgery, followed by a grimmer list if Mom did not have the surgery. And it was up to me to choose.

Only this was not *Let's Make a Deal*, where if I made the wrong choice, I went home with a case of Rice-a-Roni instead of a trip to Hawaii. This was my mother's *life*, and I was now in charge of it. How was I to decide? I am not a medical professional.

Honestly? I've always been squeamish at the sight of blood, wounds, funguses, pus, and other bodily fluids. I threw up a "Help!" prayer and asked the surgeon what she would do if it were her.

"I'd have the surgery. No question."

Mom had the surgery.

And it was a success. There were complications, however, and Mom wound up in the ICU on a ventilator. Since she had signed a Do Not Resuscitate (DNR) order and had filled out paperwork saying she didn't want to ever live on life support, the doctors explained that sometimes when they weaned patients off the ventilator, those patients stopped breathing. Did I want them to resuscitate my mother if that happened?

Another terrifying decision I had to make.

"I want you to honor her wishes," I said.

I soon found out the doctors must ask, and then ask some more, for legal reasons. As Mom's power of attorney, I had to keep answering, and they had to keep informing me of all the potential dire consequences. Every time.

They weaned my mother off the vent successfully and moved her out of ICU. Then she got pneumonia. There were other issues too. Mom grew increasingly agitated and confused and began yanking out her IV's and catheter and the tubes in her nose and throat. The nurses had to reinsert them, which was painful. After the third time, they put restraints on her arms.

Do you know how awful it is to see your mother tied to her bed like a criminal? When I returned to her room, she was trying to remove the restraints.

"Yenta Mi, take these off," she begged, breaking my heart.

My natural inclination is to jump in and fix things and make them all better, especially for the people I love. (Not always a good thing, but that is a whole other codependent story for another time.) Everything in me wanted to do what my mother asked, and the pleading in her eyes stabbed me in the heart. Tears sprang to my eyes, but I held firm.

"I can't, Mom." I stroked her hand—the one without an IV. "They're there to protect you."

"Take them off."

"I can't, Mom. I'm sorry." I tried to distract her by reading the cards from her out-of-state sisters and telling her how much everyone loved her and was praying for her. Then I stroked her hair and sang snatches of her favorite songs— "Ebbtide," "Autumn Leaves," and "The Old Rugged Cross"— which seemed to soothe her.

Five minutes later, she yanked at the restraints again. "Yenta Mi, take these off!"

Each day brought some fresh new hell. Another blockage. Another gut-wrenching decision that might result in my mother's death. Another surgery. Another setback. Then my husband and I both got sick from spending so much time in the germy hospital.

Michael came down with pneumonia, and they admitted him to the same hospital, a floor above Mom, in an isolation room. Before I could enter his room, I had to put on a hospital gown, gloves, and a mask. During my visit, a slight cough I had had for the past couple days morphed into a full-on hack attack, and the nurses made me leave.

As the day continued, my coughing got worse until I could not even speak, I was coughing so much. That night I wound up in the ER, driven there by my physician's assistant friend Susan from church. Susan was concerned I, too, might have pneumonia, so she said some magic words to the nurse in the packed emergency room, who moved me up the waiting room list.

Virginia, another friend from church, met us at the hospital and stayed with me as the minutes dragged into hours. As I lay on my ER bed hacking my lungs out and waiting for X-rays, I handed Susan my cell, so she could call Michael upstairs in his isolation room to let him know that I, too, had checked in at the same hospital Hilton along with him and Mom. After a couple hours, Susan had to leave, since she had to get up early for work in the morning, but Virginia, who is retired, remained.

Finally, at 2:30 in the morning, after wearing myself out coughing, the doctor sent me home with a diagnosis of acute bronchitis and ordered me to stay home for at least a week. The next day they released Michael from the hospital, but he was confined to bed rest for two weeks since he was still so weak.

I slept in our bedroom and Michael slept in the guest room so my incessant coughing would not keep my husband awake. At first, we would call down the hall to each other, but that made us cough too much, so we switched to texting to communicate.

Friends from church brought us meals, picked up prescriptions, and prayed for us. All the while, Mom remained in the hospital, not getting any better, with my sister and other friends and family visiting. I called the hospital twice a day to check on my mother, but I would be coughing so much, the nurses had a hard time understanding me. I kept my cell close, and they knew to call me if there was any change. Meanwhile, my sister kept me updated with texts.

One evening, I got a phone call saying Mom had aspirated on some thick liquid and I needed to come right away. Still too weak to drive, and with Michael unable to get out of bed, I called Virginia, my friend-in-shining-armor, who rushed me to the hospital. By the time I arrived, the crisis had passed, and they would not let me into Mom's room because she still had pneumonia and I was coughing too much. I stood in her doorway and called toward the direction of her bed, "I love you, Mom."

Two weeks later, I was much better, and Mom had rallied enough to go to nursing home rehab.

Except she thought she was getting to go home.

"No, Mom, not yet," I had to tell her. "You have to go to the rehab place first and get stronger, and then you can go home. You are still on IV nutrition, and they're not allowed to accept you back home with the IV. They're not equipped to deal with that."

"But I want to go home."

"I know. You will, but first you have to get stronger."

Mom did not get stronger. She declined. Rapidly. She refused to eat or get out of bed at the rehab-place-from-hell that smelled like urine and bleach. Mom grew even more confused and told visitors, "Leave me alone. I just want to sleep." She slept a lot and continued to not eat. Soon, my mother had not eaten in days and was down to eighty-two pounds.

It broke my heart to see her that way. I called my hospice-friend Annette, who lives in Texas. I had been calling and crying to Annette a lot throughout the six weeks of Mom's ordeal. I filled her in on the latest, and Annette said gently, "She's nearing the end, Laura. These are all signs of the end of life."

I knew what I had to do.

My mother was not going to die in that awful, smelly, rehab place surrounded by strangers who did not know or care about her. She was going to die at home in her own bed, in her own room, surrounded by the things she loved and the people she loved.

I called the hospice company we had used five years before, when the doctors had given Mom just days to live, and they told me the steps I needed to take to get her home fast. We jumped through several difficult hoops to make it happen, and that same night she returned home on hospice and comfort care.

Once they wheeled Mom into her room, transferred her to her bed, and covered her with the familiar floral blue quilt Michael had made her, all the tension and agitation of the past six weeks flowed out of her like melted ice cream, and she finally relaxed.

I kissed her forehead and said, "Welcome home, Mom." Then I slipped her delicate emerald-and-diamond ring back onto her finger. The ring I had been holding for safekeeping while she moved in and out of multiple rooms at the hospital.

She slowly raised her left hand up, held it in front of her, looked at her favorite ring, and smiled.

The next day, the Fourth of July, I returned to visit, but Mom was still sleeping, clearly worn out from the ordeal of the past six weeks. I kissed her hello, then sat in a chair and read while she slept, breathing heavily.

Then the Fourth of July parade began. One by one, a succession of nursing aides and other staff stopped by to say hi and tell Mom how happy they were to see her and that she was back home again.

Still, she slept on.

Her friend Margaret from down the hall came to see her, but when she saw Mom was sleeping, she visited with me for a while instead. Finally, after several hours, I had to leave to run some errands. I kissed Mom on the cheek and told her I loved her and would see her tomorrow.

The next morning at 6:20, the phone rang. I picked it up and saw the name on the caller ID. And I knew. Mom passed away peacefully in her sleep early that morning. In her own bed. In her own room. Surrounded by family photos and all the things she loved. In her own home.

When I stopped sobbing, I breathed a prayer of thanks that I was able to do that last, most important thing for my mother. Then in the quiet of the morning, in the silence I cherish, I pulled out the photo of Mom, Michael, and me on Broadway in front of the *Les Miz* sign and smiled through my tears at her happy, smiling face.

23

COMING HOME

There's no place like home.
—Dorothy, *The Wizard of Oz*

After Mom died, our Episcopal church family enfolded us in a blanket of love.

Father George conducted Mom's memorial service at her assisted living home, where we placed small bags of cookies on each chair for her friends and fellow residents with a note, saying, "Love, from the Cookie Queen." Our church friends cooked up a storm and brought platters of chicken, vegetables, salads, and desserts to the house to serve to our family and friends after the service. Our dining room table groaned under the weight of all that homemade love. We didn't need to cook for days. I was flooded with heartfelt sympathy cards, without one trite Christian platitude, and our choir family gave us a rosebush to plant in Mom's honor.

I'm so glad to be in an inclusive Episcopal church where all are welcome. Black. White. Asian. Hispanic. Single. Married. Divorced. Widowed. Democrat. Republican. Rich. Poor.

Broken. Hurting. Gay. Straight. Trans. The Jesus I know was defined by who he loved.

Jesus said, *Let us love one another, for love is of God...He who does not love does not know God, for God is love.*

I loved our church and the caring, compassionate community I had found there. It had become home, and I wanted to announce that publicly by becoming an Episcopalian. So, I signed up for confirmation class, as did Michael. After completing the class, we went through the sacramental rite of confirmation and made a formal commitment of faith to be received into the Episcopal Church.

It was Pastor Mary's final confirmation class. Several months before, she had announced her upcoming retirement. When we first heard Pastor Mary would be leaving, we were dismayed and saddened. We adored her as our rector, and she and her husband Paul had become good friends. They were the reason we began attending that church in the first place.

In fact, Michael had become a member of the same community theater group based at the church as Paul, and they'd had a lot of fun acting together in a Neil Simon comedy. In the going-away photo album gift the theater group presented to Paul, Michael wrote to his friend, "I'd been wandering in the darkness for a few years, and way in the distance I saw a light; though I couldn't see the path, I could see the light, and kept walking towards it. The light was Jesus, and you were holding it, guiding me home to [this church.]"

There's no place like home.

Nearly a year and a half after Pastor Mary retired, our beloved Father George, who conducted my mother's memorial service and who had also become a dear friend, announced his retirement. I felt sad all over again, but we never thought of leaving the church. Unlike most of the evangelical churches we had attended in the past, where a huge part of the church's popularity is due to its pastor, I'd learned the Episcopal Church is *not* the clergy.

We are all the church, and we will continue to be the church. Together.

Another thing our Episcopal church has taught me is that not all retreats are the same. Shortly after joining the choir, I discovered they had an annual fall retreat to get away and practice the music for the upcoming season, and to have a fun bonding time together. My choir mates encouraged me to go, but I explained I wasn't a retreat girl.

Not my cup of tea.

My musical friends wore me down until I finally gave in. To my surprise, I had a good time in that gorgeous woodland setting.

I loved the camaraderie during rehearsal, the learning of more beautiful music together, and the great food prepared by the kitchen staff. I loved hanging out with my friends, shopping in the quirky stores of the tiny nearby town, and playing Pictionary/charades after rehearsal Saturday night, where the women skunked the men. At least that's how I remember it.

Yet the rustic sleeping stuff still didn't work for me. I bunked with three of my friends in one room with the ubiquitous bunk beds.

At least these beds had plastic mattresses that could be disinfected with bleach wipes, so I wouldn't have to worry about sleeping on the dead skin of hundreds of other campers before me.

The only problem: I brought a fitted sheet that wouldn't stay on the plastic mattress. It kept sliding off throughout the night, so I woke up repeatedly, my shivering skin touching the cold plastic and desperately needing to go to the bathroom. Which, of course, our four-star rustic cabin didn't have.

Teeth chattering and bladder ready to burst, I threw on a coat and shoes, grabbed my flashlight, and tentatively made my way through the inky darkness down to the women's restroom, terrified the entire way. Certain I'd surprise a scary skunk or possum in my path. Really having fun now.

Once I heeded the call of Mother Nature, I had to make my way back again, through all the wilderness and critters hiding in the blackness, to my cabin. Because we love our choir family, Michael and I plan to attend the annual retreat again.

But next time, we're sleeping at a B&B in town.

I am a big fan of sleeping, particularly since the Nazi nightmare disappeared years ago and hasn't returned. When we first got married, I would kick my husband in my sleep as I tried to evade the storm troopers chasing me in their heavy boots.

Michael would gently wake me and say, "Honey, I'm not a Nazi."

Not too long after that, the nightmares stopped for good.

I may not be great at a lot of the spiritual disciplines—daily Bible reading, meditating, fasting—but I excel at napping. There is a lot to be said for the restorative spiritual power of naps, which is why I take one every Sunday afternoon.

Cuddling with our rescue spaniel-mix Mellie (our beloved Gracie crossed the rainbow bridge a few years ago) is another one of my spiritual practices. As I gaze into our canine-daughter's soulful brown eyes shining with unconditional love, my soul expands and my heart floods with joy.

Thank you, God, for dogs.

I also try to practice gratitude on a regular basis. I began this practice in the hospital after puking my guts out from chemo. I needed to get my mind off the worry and anxiety of when my next retch session might happen.

Instead of focusing on the awfulness that I knew would come again, I redirected my thoughts to thankfulness and began writing down what I was thankful for:

- Being alive
- Bernadette Peters singing "Being Alive"
- Michael's comforting arms
- A husband who kept his "in sickness and in health" marriage vows
- God's love
- A sister who gave me shots to help bring my blood cell counts back to normal
- Heated blankets
- Mammograms
- My breast-cancer survivor mother
- My father who taught me to dream
- Books
- Laughter
- Compassionate nurses
- The ocean
- Kindred spirits
- Friends who gave me pretty hats and scarves to keep my bald head warm
- England
- Afternoon naps
- Music that lifts up my soul
- Mandy Patinkin singing "Lily's Eyes"
- Colm Wilkinson's "Bring Him Home"
- Kristin Chenoweth and Idina Menzel singing "For Good"
- When Fantine, Eponine, and Jean Valjean sing "and remember the truth that once was spoken, to love another person is to see the face of God"

Now, I would add to that list our neighborhood Episcopal church.

24

LUMPS, JUST YOUR AVERAGE
NEUROSES, AND COLIN FIRTH

*...A man who has never been afflicted with a neurosis
does not know the meaning of suffering.*
—Henry Miller

In my late fifties, I had my remaining boob removed after finding another lump (precancerous) and undergoing genetic testing, which revealed I have a mutation of the BRCA-2 gene, putting me at increased risk for breast cancer. That's when I decided to go flat. Breasts don't make a woman.

Before the surgeon sliced off my second breast, I held a "Bye-Bye Booby" party with a group of friends in the back room of my favorite Mexican restaurant.

"To symmetry!" I said, raising my margarita glass high.

"To symmetry," my girlfriends chorused.

As I swallowed the salt crystals and tequila, I glanced down at my cleavage, admiring the soft curve of my remaining breast. Then I copped a quick feel. A farewell hug.

After dinner we enjoyed "Nipples of Venus"—white cupcakes with white frosting and a cherry on top—for dessert, courtesy of my friend Connie.

Here's what I shared on Facebook after my surgery.

Surgery went great! It doesn't even feel like I've had surgery—no pain. Amazing. I feel really good and so relieved that it's behind me.

There were a couple emotional things and some confusion at the last minute that resulted in increased anxiety and tears—the last thing I wanted right before surgery—but that disappeared when I woke up alive and not puking from the anesthesia. A first.

I've been on a high ever since. The drugs might be a factor.

I won't get the pathology results* for a week, but my surgeon said the lymph nodes looked "good," so I'm feeling much better about it, and the fear of cancer is now gone, thanks to God and the power of prayer—all your prayers.

I'm no longer even going to think about those results until the day the doc tells me what they are. Instead, I'm celebrating the success of the surgery and the fact that I'm alive!

Another great outcome of the surgery is that the sadness and grieving I had been feeling about the upcoming loss of my breast has disappeared. Poof. Gone.

Also, something about hearing from three different nurses— including an oncology nurse who frequently works with breast cancer patients—that nearly fifty percent of the women who have recon- structive surgery develop infections, other complications, and further surgeries as a result of that plastic surgery and having a foreign object in their body.

All just to have breasts? Fatty tissue whose only "function" is to feed babies? Something I have never had and will not be having at this age. I don't think so. Not this woman.

I am not my breasts.

*(The pathology results came back clear. No cancer. I did have several precancerous areas, however, so I'm relieved I got rid of that puppy.)

I am my eyes that see beauty in a field of daffodils, a crimson sunset, a starry night, a child's curls, and a good book. (Who knew that the pain meds they gave me would make me so deep? Eloquent, too. Move over, Virginia Woolf.)

I am my ears that delight in the rustling of the wind through the trees, the sounds of the sea, the giggles of a child, and Kristin Chenoweth and Idina Menzel singing "For Good."

I am my mouth that loves singing, storytelling, good long talks with girlfriends, the taste of salmon, a great steak, juicy watermelon, chocolate, a perfect cup of English tea, and my husband's kisses.

I am my arms that can hug a friend, enfold a child, embrace my beloved, hold a book, and snuggle with our Mellie-girl.

I am spirit and soul filled with gratitude, freedom, and God's love.

And I am love and laughter, creativity, sorrow, and neuroses. In short, a woman. A writer. A human being. Not a breast.

Reconstruction is a very personal decision for each woman. Perhaps if I were single and younger, I might choose differently. But I'm fast approaching sixty, and lucky to be married to a man who adores me. All of me.

Again, breasts are just fatty tissue. (I've probably lost five pounds with the removal of this second one—yay!) Most importantly, I do not want to have further surgery, anesthesia, or be cut again for something unnecessary.

When I next have surgery, it is going to be for something preventive, medically necessary, or to save my life. Not get cosmetic surgery to gain boobs and "feel like a woman," or "attractive."

Despite what Hollywood and pop culture would have us believe, it's not all about the cleavage. I've chosen to embrace my flatness.

Only…it's not just flat; it's concave where my second breast used to be. I now have a cavern in my chest. Truthfully? It's more than a cavern. It's the bloody Grand Canyon. (I can say bloody because I was stationed in England years ago.)

But that's okay. I'm alive. And after all, the Grand Canyon is one of the seven natural wonders of the world.

Three months after my second mastectomy, I said goodbye to my ovaries with an "oophorectomy." My BRCA-2 gene mutation also puts me at increased risk for ovarian cancer, and since there is no good test for ovarian cancer, doctors recommend removing the ovaries and fallopian tubes as the best preventive measure.

Works for me. I do not need any of those lady parts anymore—I am a post-menopausal woman.

My gynecologist did say that their removal might increase the amount of testosterone in my body. When I relayed that to Michael, he said dryly, "What? You're going to become *more* assertive?"

I am grateful for a husband who did not marry me for my breasts. Michael married me for my independence, my artistic nature, sense of humor, and killer scrambled eggs.

I thank God every day for a man who believes in and takes his marriage vows seriously. *For better or worse, for richer or poorer, in sickness and in health...*

The first test of those vows came on our honeymoon when we made love. Yes, we waited until the wedding night. (Back in our evangelical days we believed sex was a gift from God and you didn't open the gift until after the wedding.)

After waiting for this special moment for nearly six months, we were both more than eager to open the gift. Our coupling was tender and loving, and increasingly passionate. Everything was going great until I began to hyperventilate.

"Are you okay?" my beloved asked.

I shook my head and pushed my hands against his chest—that massive, heavy male chest that was crushing me and pinning me to the bed.

"Can't breathe," I gasped.

Instantly, he rolled off me. I gulped in a huge breath and released it. Then another.

"I'm sorry," I said, beginning to cry. "I don't know what's wrong."

But we both did. My beloved knew about the-thing-that-must-not-be-named.

"It's okay," Michael said as he stroked my cheek. He kissed my tears away, gently cupped my face between his hands and gazed into my eyes with more tenderness and devotion than I have ever known. "I love you. We have our whole lives together. Besides," he added with a sly grin, "we're both creative types, so I'm sure we can figure something out."

We did.

Thank God that fundamentalist fiancé kicked me to the curb all those years ago. If he hadn't, I would never have gotten my genuine happily ever after.

That does not mean my marriage to Michael is always sunshine, puppy dogs, and daffodils. Two strong-minded artistic types living under the same roof can create sporadic drama.

After thirty years of marriage, we occasionally—more than occasionally—have miscommunication issues. Michael can get on my last nerve, and vice versa. We may not see eye to eye on everything, but both agree that we will never drive in Europe again. (See below.)

For all our quirks and differences, at the end of the day, there is still no one I would rather come home to.

Confession: I am a tiny bit of a control freak. I've also inherited my mother's Miller family trait of wanting (needing) my house to always (most of the time) be clean and tidy. Cleanliness is next to godliness, after all. There's nothing like the smell of Lemon Pledge on a Saturday morning.

The two of us.

Part of it is that midwestern work ethic instilled in me at an early age. I had the typical messy bedroom of a teenager, but once I joined the Air Force, that messiness was drilled out of me. Now I crave order and tidiness. I need everything to be in its proper place. And I still fold my underwear into equal thirds. Thanks, Uncle Sam.

Michael teases me with that Kathy Bates line from *Misery*, "The penguin always faces north!"

When we first got married and Michael's family would come over to visit, often, when I left the living room, his twin teenaged nieces would move books and knickknacks on the fireplace mantel, so that they were slightly off-kilter. I would return to the room, rejoin the conversation, and while talking, automatically adjust the book or knickknack back to its proper angle as the twins burst out laughing.

Call me compulsive.

What was once a cute and endearing trait has grown less cute over time. I have an obsessive need for everything to be clean and tidy, both inside and out. Saturday mornings while

Michael sleeps in, I often wake up at 6:30, go into the backyard, and quietly start weeding and deadheading so as not to awaken my husband or the neighbors. I wait until eight o'clock, the legally acceptable hour for making noise, to start raking and sweeping the leaves that drop from the myriad trees onto the hardpan earth in our secret garden. I even sweep the dirt. It's important to have a neat ground surface.

Problem is, I don't know when to stop. Whenever Michael and I go out on the patio to have a cool drink and relax together, we'll be chatting away when I suddenly jump up to pick up a few stray leaves, deadhead a rosebush, or move a flowerpot just so.

Once, the former office where I used to work (all scientists except for our administrative assistant and writer me) went on a field trip through a river preserve. We traipsed down worn paths through marshes and native grasses to view the ecosystem restoration that had been done.

At least that's what they said we were doing.

All I saw was dirt; a bunch of dead, dry grass; lots of weeds; and ugly brown withered plants that no one had bothered to deadhead. Since I did not have my trusty pruning shears with me, I reached up and snapped off a couple of the dead, dry flowers next to me.

There. Much better.

"Laura, don't do that!" one of the scientists said.

Evidently not. She explained that they never disturb the vegetation but simply let it go, allowing it to die and drop off naturally, where it decomposes and becomes natural compost, then blooms again in season.

I still think it looks better tidied up.

Some people who know and love me think that I am the tiniest bit neurotic. Others call me high maintenance, like Sally in

When Harry Met Sally, due to my precise eating habits. Like Sally, I just want my food the way I want it.

Hot foods should always be hot and cold foods or drinks, cold. None of this lukewarm, in-between stuff. Additionally, scrambled eggs must always be on a separate plate from pancakes so the syrup (HOT, not mealy-mouthed room temperature) does not ooze onto the eggs. Syrup must *never* touch eggs.

Food is not my only issue.

I have had a problem with noise since I was a kid. I cannot stand loud music, revving motorcycles, overhead bathroom fans, dripping faucets, or blaring TV's. Especially commercials, football games, and reality TV shows. Too much yelling and screaming for my delicate ears.

As a kid at family holiday gatherings, I would hide under the dining room table with my nose in a book to escape the sounds of my male relatives, crowded around the television watching the football game and yelling. It also kept me away from child labor in the kitchen with the women.

As I grew older, my noise intolerance was aggravated by PMS, so I named it PMSNI (PMS noise irritation). That PMSNI went off the charts a few times. Once, during my single days, my friend Luke—one of my many platonic pals from the megachurch with the huge singles group—began stirring concentrated orange juice in a plastic pitcher with a wooden spoon. The repetitive noise of the spoon hitting the hard sides of the pitcher, *ker-thump-thump*, *ker-thump-thump*, *ker-thump-thump*, drove me insane.

Finally, I turned on Luke in a frenzy and snarled, "*Must* you make that noise?"

No wonder he never wanted to date me.

I haven't had PMS in years, but I still have an extreme sensitivity to noise. Heavy metal and hard rock make me want to gouge out my eyes, while rap makes me want to gouge out my eyes and pull up their pants.

My friends and family members under fifty roll their eyes at what they perceive as my unhip, old-lady-like aversion to their music, but I don't care. I have never been hip. (See Chapter Three.)

Thanks to TV morning show host Kelly Ripa, I learned that my sensitivity to noise is an actual physical condition called misophonia: a hatred of sound.

When I looked misophonia up online, I discovered that those who suffer from this disorder usually respond in one of two ways: fight or flight. According to the article, they either become enraged and potentially violent, or get anxious and run away.

Ha! Take that my hipster friends and family. IT HAS A NAME. More than one, in fact. A while ago, a friend sent me an article about "Highly Sensitive Persons" (HSPs), people who cannot stand noise and need plenty of sleep and quiet places to retreat to, among other things.

C'est moi.

Who knew I was a highly sensitive person? I thought I was just high maintenance and old.

On her morning show, Kelly said the sound of chewing drives her up the wall, so she's taught her kids to eat quietly, but the noise of her husband eating a juicy peach can make her leave the house.

My misophonia is not quite that bad, but you'll never find revving motorcycles, heavy metal, or reality TV in our house.

My neuroses followed me overseas. About a decade ago, Michael and I finally got the chance to return to Europe on vacation again. Something we had been longing to do since our last trip several years earlier. Our itinerary started with a pilgrimage to Canterbury Cathedral, followed by visits to Bruges, Paris, and Normandy, and ended with a return to southern England to see our dear friends in Dorset.

The month before we left the states, the West African Ebola epidemic was at its peak and had been declared an international public health emergency. Ebola hysteria was spreading like a red wine stain on a white tablecloth through the media and causing concerns among travelers.

I'd also read that the huge African migrant population in Calais, France, had recently rioted in their attempts to get into England, so I had this tiny fear hardly worth mentioning that after getting off the ferry in Calais, we might catch Ebola from the huddled masses striving to break free. I packed extra hand sanitizer.

Then there was the terrible beheading of an American journalist in Syria by a terrorist who was a Brit and the subsequent raising of England's terror alert to severe, meaning a terrorist attack was "highly likely." It didn't help when one week before we left on vacation, England's prime minister said Britain faced the "greatest and deepest terror threat in the country's history."

Really excited to be traveling right then.

One of my writer friends, who was slated to travel to England a week after us to do research on a book, cancelled her trip over her family's concerns for her safety. But this was our dream trip we had been longing to take for years. No way we were going to cancel.

Michael doesn't pay as much attention to the media as I do, but as a former journalist, I can't help myself. I was bombarded daily on all sides by the fearmongering in the news and, consequently, became just a teensy bit nervous. Convinced we might not make it home alive, I arranged to have friends from church adopt our sweet spaniel-mix Mellie so she would go to a good home. I also mailed my magnum opus—an earlier version of this book—to my agent, my priest, and select friends and family, so that it would not die along with me.

A few days before we left, I gave my eager traveler husband a loving smile and said, "Aren't you happy that I'm not freaking out over all these Ebola and terrorist concerns and insisting we cancel our trip?"

"Very."

Except I was freaking out. Big time.

I didn't want to tell Michael and spoil the trip. Instead, I said in a jokey voice, "Well, since I'm not being all neurotic and fearful, you have to promise to always stay with me, especially in France, since I don't speak the language." Images from *Taken* and Liam Neeson's teenage daughter kidnapped by human traffickers in Paris flashed before me. Although I had left my teens decades ago, it was always good to be cautious.

Reluctantly, Michael agreed to my jokey request, but only because we had run into a last-minute snafu and would have just one workable cell phone between us.

My husband did not have a clue how strong and how deep my fears were. I did not realize until recently that the root of all my fears was the-thing-that-must-not-be-named. All roads lead back to that.

Convinced that terrorists were going to bomb the Paris Metro or the London Tube, leaving us blown to bits or worse, trapped underground, I insisted that we walk or take cabs instead. On a requisite train trip through the English country-side, I was certain that the foreign men across the aisle from us were planning an attack. They kept looking around furtively and speaking excitedly in a language I didn't recognize. I never left my seat. Instead, I remained glued to Michael's side, knowing that at least we would die together. Complete with a full bladder.

Our long-planned dream vacation became a nightmare. Something about one of us being consumed by fear and myriad things going wrong. Like…losing our railway tickets and having to buy new ones. Not being able to find an ATM to get Euros for the public bathrooms in France when we first arrived with full-to-bursting bladders. And my struggling with the stick shift we rented in Normandy. Michael had to take the wheel while I tried to navigate. Directionally impaired *moi*. In French. The only French I know is *Bonjour Monsieur, Au Revoir mon ami, crepes, éclairs,* and *Bouef Bourguignon*—said in Julia Child's voice.

We soon discovered that all French road signs are set at an angle, so when you think you are supposed to turn right or left, instead, you are supposed to go straight. We spent fifty-six minutes driving around in circles in the Normandy city of Rouen down one-way streets trying to find our hotel, which our phone GPS kept showing us was just a block away. Following the GPS, we wound up driving on the cathedral sidewalk, scattering pedestrians in our wake. After that clueless and embarrassing American debacle, we finally parked in a car park and walked to our hotel, a mere half block away. In that lovely hotel, next to the beautiful Rouen cathedral famously painted by Monet, I spent the entire night in the bathroom with a horrible case of Napoleon's revenge. Who knew you should never ask for ice in your Coke in the French countryside?

Good times.

But the worst part of the trip came on the ferry from Cherbourg, France, to Poole, England. The perfect place to plant a bomb. It would take out both English and French citizens as well as unlucky Western tourists like us. Michael and I had tickets for seats next to each other on the four-and-a-half-hour ferry trip, but when we approached our designated section, an elderly couple had taken our spots in the row of three seats so they could sit next to each other, rather than split up.

Good Christian that I am, I shot daggers at the older

couple's oblivious hunched backs and directed uncharitable thoughts their way. *What? Just because you're old, you think that gives you more right to die together side by side than my beloved and me? Hey, I went through a lot of creeps before I found my Renaissance man. I'm not going to be blown to bits for eternity without his hand in mine. We deserve our happily ever after just as much as you!*

Michael, being the kind and gracious person he is, decided we would split up instead, and he would sit behind me.

"Oh no you won't," I hissed. "We have to sit next to each other."

"Why? I'll be right behind you."

"So, I can be holding your hand in case something happens."

"Like what?"

That's when I spilled out all my neurotic, pent-up fears, revealing that terrorists planting a bomb on our ferry made perfect sense. My beloved, who was already a bit twitchy and unhappy from having to stay cooped up in our tiny, muggy Paris hotel room while I napped, snapped, "Your neuroses are smothering me."

Not a high-water mark in our marriage.

Deciding that asking my husband to hold my hand at that moment might be pushing it, I took the high road. I suggested instead that Michael go out on deck and explore the four-story ferry to his heart's content.

Once he left, I was alone and didn't know another soul on board the massive ship. Trying not to panic that terrorists might attack in my beloved's absence, I said a quick prayer and settled in with my Colin Firth biography, attempting to fill my overanxious gray matter with images of the inestimable Colin as Mr. Darcy, in his white shirt, coming out of the pond at Pemberley.

Once we arrived safely in England, I relaxed and tried to make light of my neurotic tendencies, joking and telling on myself to our dear English friends David and Patricia. They laughed and agreed I was being too neurotic and allowing the American media fear mongering to get to me. Yet Patricia, a lifelong Brit who always tells it like it is, vindicated my fears when she agreed she would never take the London Underground either.

"Oh no," she said. "First place they'd attack."

Ha! I'm not the neurotic lone ranger after all. Of course, Patricia's severe asthma is the actual reason she does not ride the Tube.

25

DIGGING UP THE DEEP

We bury things so deep we no longer
remember there was anything to bury.
Our bodies remember. Our neurotic states remember.
But we don't.
—Jeanette Winterson

After walking away from the writing and publishing world more than a decade ago (the same time we walked away from the evangelical church), totally burned out and not knowing, or caring, if I ever wrote again, I ended up talking to my writer friend Cindy. I told her how much we loved our new Episcopal church, and she said, "You should write a spiritual memoir."

Really? *Me?* But I'm not that spiritual.

I liked the sound of it and scratched down a few notes, then set it aside. Months later, I picked up the manuscript, wrote a few more paragraphs, came up with an appropriately spiritual title—*Finding Church Again*—and mentioned to my retiring rector and friend Pastor Mary what I was writing. Then I set it aside again.

Several months later, when Pastor Mary and her husband Paul came to dinner, she asked how my spiritual memoir was coming along. I confessed I'd gotten sidetracked and stopped working on it. The next day, I picked up my pen again and the writing flowed.

I rediscovered my writing passion and could not wait to get home from my soul-sucking government job each day to write about something that interested me and had meaning. When I finished my first draft, I showed it to a couple editor friends who liked it but suggested that since it was a *spiritual* memoir, it should focus more on my spiritual "journey." Everything in the book needed to point to that journey and move it forward.

If I had realized that I'd been on a spiritual journey, I wouldn't have brought along so much baggage.

My friends suggested I read other spiritual memoirs for guidance. I did and tried to follow the spiritual memoir parameters. I struggled to think profound spiritual thoughts; sprinkled Scripture throughout; wove in quotes from theologians and other deep, spiritual people; deleted funny, unspiritual rabbit trails; and tried to be more introspective and gaze deeply at my navel.

Only I couldn't see my navel for my stomach fat, and I really wanted to watch *Fixer Upper* with Chip and Joanna.

I tried my best to follow the spiritual memoir formula and failed. My book was rejected again and again, and I looked for the nearest razor blade. Then I heard about a young, bestselling author, whose spiritual memoir about leaving the evangelical church for the more progressive Episcopal church was about to be released. Her book even had "finding church" in the title, and I knew I was toast. Burnt toast.

My first thought was, *She stole my memoir!* But I knew that wasn't very Christian, so after a few days of whining, and with a friend's wise guidance, I reframed it to, "We're not the same person or the same age. We each have our own spiritual journey and bring something different to the table. Both our stories are valid." That's the adult, got-it-all-together response. By this age, I would like to think I finally have it all together.

I would also like to think I have thin thighs and no double chin.

The thing is, I'm not a deeply spiritual person; I'm only sort-of spiritual. I'm no theologian, eschatologist, or scholar of all things spiritual. I haven't gone to seminary and have no desire to do so.

My faith is simpler.

To me, God has always been like air. Or gravity. Something I can't see but know is there. God keeps me alive and grounded. God never leaves me.

God the Father filled that huge empty hole in my heart left by my father's death. God comforted me when my fundamentalist fiancé dumped me a week before our wedding. And God was with me in that fraternity room on that awful night. I just didn't know it at the time.

In the movie *Notting Hill*, Julia Roberts says to Hugh Grant, "I'm just a girl, standing in front of a boy, asking him to love her." I'm just a girl (can you still be a girl in your sixties?) who, after years of feeling ashamed and not good enough and searching and looking for love, safety, and a place to belong, has finally found it. That, and acceptance.

I scratched the first draft of my memoir and started over.

After reading the second draft, one of my dear friends, who has known me a long time, gently asked that if in addition to the brief recounting of the-thing-that-must-not-be-named I had included, whether I might consider expanding on it and showing how that awful night in the fraternity room had impacted my life.

"Nope." Not in this universe, baby.

I did *not* want to go there. I'm the lighthearted, funny woman who is not big on introspection, so my succinct description of that ancient painful history was enough for me. I was *over it* and did not want to attach any more significance or importance to that long-ago event and bog down my now humorous "good-girl-gone-bad-gone-good-again" memoir. (What's up with that whole good-girl thing anyway? Time to rethink that outdated label.)

Humor has always been my go-to coping mechanism. That's how I got through breast cancer and later used my experience to write a book about fighting cancer with faith, hope, and a healthy dose of laughter. Another book that got rejected repeatedly. Fourteen times, but who's counting?

Publishers at the time (mostly conservative white Christian males) were uncomfortable with the idea of cancer and humor, especially b-b-b-breast cancer. "You can't have cancer and humor," they said.

Really? Have *you* had cancer? Because that's how I made it through that awful time. So did many other women. When I was writing my breast cancer book, I met with a group of women who'd all survived the big C and some who were still undergoing treatment. We laughed, cried, and swapped stories of bad wigs, all-over hair loss, reconstruction, radiation tattoos, and breast forms falling out in the most inconvenient places. Like other people's swimming pools.

Cancer isn't funny, but humor is healing. The humor in that little pink book—which eventually got published, thanks to a now-retired editor named Lonnie—has helped many women through their cancer journey, for which I'm grateful. I'm also grateful that the publisher released a revised, updated edition of *Thanks for the Mammogram!* two decades later, with a killer cover that cracked me up when I saw it: white Nipples of Venus cupcakes against a fuchsia-pink background. So funny.

There's nothing funny about the-thing-that-must-not-be-named, however, and this author doesn't usually do serious.

Therefore, a brief mention of that awful night in the fraternity house was good enough for me.

What I didn't tell my friend who suggested I expand upon my sexual assault and its aftereffects was how difficult it was for me to even write the few paragraphs I had. To relive that painful memory and put it down on paper for the whole world to see, knowing that people would look at me differently and judge me. People I knew and liked, admired, respected, even loved. People who knew me only as the nice, middle-aged bookworm and rabid Anglophile who loves tea, sings in the church choir, and used to write fun-and-fluffy books.

I did not want that one traumatic event to forever define me. I knew it was important to be honest and transparent when writing a memoir, but I thought a quick recounting of that shocking, life-changing thing-that-must-not-be-named would be sufficient.

It wasn't.

Yet I still was not ready to consider it, examine it, or address the elephant in the room. I set the memoir aside.

Overall, I have a good life. I know that and am grateful. I'm healthy (apart from that extra weight I carry around like a security blanket); married to my best friend; recently retired from cubicle world (hallelujah!), with a modest pension and health benefits; writing again; and have good friends and family, the world's most adorable and affectionate dog, a cozy little cottage, and a kind, loving church we now call home.

Many are not as fortunate, including some whom I know and love.

Some have gone through unwanted, painful divorces. Others have endured the heartbreaking loss of a loved one, while still others have found themselves hit with major health issues, causing them to lose their jobs and become unemployable, resulting in financial devastation that has left them living on the edge after a lifetime of hard work in what was supposed to be their golden years. In comparison, (yes, I know we're not supposed to compare, but I'm making a point) my life is a cakewalk.

A few years ago, however, I went through a difficult patch with lots of losses, as my therapist pointed out to me when I vented about a bad day at work, an unexpected financial setback, and some extended family difficulties. I had been grumpy and out of sorts for a while and couldn't figure out why. Those losses, in concert with the increase in deadly mass shootings, random terror attacks, and general nastiness of the latest political season, had taken a toll. (Confession: I used to roll my eyes when celebrities and others mentioned their therapists; wrongly thinking therapy was a self-indulgent, navel-gazing, practice. I've since seen the light and am more grateful than I can say for the help and healing therapists have provided to me and those I love.)

All my life I've been an optimist, a hopeful idealist who sees the glass as half-full, an impulsive *Carpe Diem* person brimming with dreams and ideas, who eagerly chases her passions and pie-in-the-sky fantasies and bounces back swiftly from letdowns and setbacks. During those years, my glass had been drained until it was bone-dry, and I had a hard time refilling it.

"You're depressed," my therapist said.

"I don't get depressed." Usually. Not this resilient, pull-myself-up-by-the-bootstraps woman who moves on and gets over failures and disappointments quickly.

Apparently, it was no surprise I was depressed after all the losses I had suffered in a relatively short span of time. My therapist ticked them off on her fingers, beginning with my breast, ovaries, and fallopian tubes, and said I was grieving those losses and needed to allow myself time to grieve and heal.

Except I did not grieve the loss of my breast. It's just fatty tissue.

Not a child. Not a husband. Both of whom had been lost by people I loved. Those loved ones were going through deep, immobilizing pain and grief. The kind that is a raw, open wound. The gutted, heartbreaking kind that makes it impossible to breathe. In comparison, the loss of a boob was nothing. My mind and heart knew that.

My body was another story.

Mentally and emotionally, I was fine, and off-the-charts relieved, by the removal of my breast and other lady parts. But it took a while for my body to recover from two surgeries that were only three months apart.

This decisive fix-it woman took quick action to solve the problem that had the potential to become dangerous, even fatal, down the road. I moved fast to prevent cancer from getting the chance to invade and take control of my body again. I was *not* going to let that happen. I just didn't realize that my then nearly-sixty-year-old body would not bounce back and heal as quickly from the surgery as I expected.

My healer friend Annette explained it to me: I was cut by a knife. Twice. In a short time frame. Even though skilled surgeons performed the cuts in a professional and sterile environment, and even though the downstairs second surgery was laparoscopic, the flesh still responds to an "attack" from a knife. It is a violation against the body, she said, and the human body reacts accordingly and needs time to heal.

Two weeks after that second surgery, I returned to work and a new position in another government agency. It was too much, too soon. I wasn't fully recovered yet and I was worn out. I made it through the first day of work but felt a tickle in my throat. That night I came down with a combination of flu and bronchitis. All night long, I hacked my lungs out and ran a fever. I was forced to call in sick the next day and the next. I wound up staying home the rest of the week. Way to make a great impression on my new supervisor.

Then, over the next six months, one personal or professional crisis and loss after another hit, causing me to withdraw and retreat. I was unhappy, depressed, negative, whiny, and tired of being depressed. I missed myself—that hopeful, optimistic woman who chased her dreams with gusto and bounced back quickly from hard knocks.

Except I wasn't bouncing back this time.

My therapist's words kept returning to me, and as I took the time to honestly consider them and mull them over, I realized that the cumulative losses over the past few years *had* taken a toll, and I had been grieving without knowing it. Then my dear friend's words about the-thing-that-must-not-be-named that happened when I was nineteen returned, and I began mulling them over as well.

Her words made me recall what another first-reader friend had said after she reviewed an early draft of this memoir. She, too, remarked on how I had skirted around the hard parts. This was after I had hesitantly and nervously inserted my concise recounting of the-thing-that-must-not-be-named. A huge, scary thing that had been buried and hidden for decades, something I had considered writing about in my forties but ultimately decided against after a couple publishing friends gently asked, "Are you sure you want that in print? Once it is out there for everyone to read, you will be forever labeled as 'that woman who was raped.'"

Major hyperventilating pause. I did not want to be labeled by the-thing-that-must-not-be-named. The thing I was about to name before the entire world. I didn't want that to become my whole identity. I am *not* the awful thing that happened to me. I am so much more than that. Woman. Child of God. Wife. Writer. Friend. Sister. Niece. Aunt. Dog mom. Dreamer. Reader. Anglophile.

Yes, I wanted (needed) to write about what had happened, *some*day, but fifteen-plus years ago, when I was first thinking of doing so, I released a huge sigh of relief when my publishing pals talked me out of it. I decided that I would write about the-thing-that-must-not-be-named at some point, but I would disguise the trauma in a novel instead—a work of fiction. That way, I could still express myself and my feelings about that awful episode yet fly under the radar and remain invisible.

Invisible is good, particularly for a private person like me. (Don't laugh. Believe it or not, I am private and introverted at heart.) What is not good is ignoring and running away from the ramifications of that long-ago night.

My first-reader friend who said I had skirted around the hard parts knew about my sexual assault but not the details. Nor did she know how hard it was for me to reveal those details on paper. I had dashed off those dreaded particulars and then moved on to the rest of the book. When I asked my harried young friend, amid multiple deadlines she then had, what she thought of that shocking scene and how people might react to it, I held my breath in fearful anticipation. She replied that it wouldn't be as shocking today due to how common the issue of campus rape had become in the past few years, and how much more it has been made a part of the public consciousness.

Campus rape may be common and much more talked about today, but it was an uncommon, terrifying experience for me back in the seventies. One that I now finally realize colored the rest of my life and had lasting repercussions. Something I clearly did not bounce back from quickly or get over, as much as I tried to convince myself otherwise over the years.

I know, believe, and say aloud the words, "Rape is NOT the woman's fault," but I now see that I had bought into that age-old, deep-seated cultural notion that the woman is to blame. Particularly when she is not a virgin and a gun or knife is not

LAURA JENSEN WALKER

involved. I also realized that I still felt shame over what happened to me more than forty-five years ago. Forty-five years.

I should never have put myself in that situation. I should never have drunk so much that I passed out. And in that falling-down-drunk state, I should never have accepted what seemed to my nineteen-year-old, alcohol-fogged brain a polite, chivalrous offer to drive me home. What did I expect?

I didn't expect rape.

Sexual assault is an epidemic on college campuses today. It was prevalent in my day and long before; we just did not talk about it. Thankfully, more and more gutsy young women today are coming forward and speaking out. Like the Stanford rape victim who wrote the powerful twelve-page letter to her attacker, telling him how that night destroyed her life. I was moved by the bravery and eloquence of this young woman's letter that began: *"You don't know me, but you've been inside me..."*

I wasn't the only one. Journalist Ashleigh Banfield spent more than half of her hour-long CNN show reading the letter aloud. Members of both parties of Congress read aloud the full statement on the floor of the House of Representatives, officially putting the young victim's words into the congressional record. President Joe Biden, who wrote the 1994 Violence Against Women Act, and was involved in the "It's On Us" campaign against campus sexual assault, wrote an emotional online response to that brave young woman when he was Vice President, saying her words were "forever seared" on his soul and that those words should be required reading for men and women of all ages.

That brave young woman's articulate, affecting letter was viewed more than thirteen million times online. As I read the rest of her letter, one sentence jumped out and spoke directly to me: *"Sometimes I think, if I hadn't gone, then this never would've happened. But then I realized, it would have happened, just to some-body else."*

If I hadn't...

During recovery at home, after surgery for a torn meniscus, I spent a lot of time reading and thinking about rape and its lasting effects. Statistics say one in five women will be sexually assaulted in their lifetime. I realized that it is time to stop being ashamed and blaming myself for what happened to me when I was nineteen. It's time for this sixty-five-year-old woman to speak out too.

I picked the memoir back up and began writing again.

At last, I was finally ready to think about and examine the lasting impacts of that long-ago night. Impacts like my continual need to be in control and resistance to anyone—particularly men—who tries to control me. That topped the list, followed close behind by my fear of feeling trapped. Not just in isolated cabins in the woods, confined spaces like caves, and too-crowded elevators, but even in social and work situations.

For instance, a few years ago, I was forced (which got things off wrong from the start) to attend a weeklong work training event at a conference grounds two hours from home. Forced to also carpool with coworkers in the work van, rather than drive myself, left me no way to escape the conference grounds, if need be, which also meant it left me trapped with a group of strangers on those unfamiliar grounds.

Deep breaths, deep breaths.

Once we arrived, I only knew three people out of the work group of fifty or so. A group of cliquish, outdoorsy friends who had worked together and bonded over their mutual job interests for years. A job interest I did not share, using technology I was unfamiliar with and had difficulty understanding. (Technology, like math, has never been a strong suit for this right-brained woman.) Talk about a fish out of water. Stranger in a strange land. Alien. Misfit. Dinosaur.

Good times.

I tried to connect with some of my coworkers by discussing books, movies, or travel at meals in the communal dining room, but those attempts quickly fizzled out as the outdoorsy group returned to their common core work conversations. A foreign language to me, since as the token indoorsy writer, I didn't do the same job. I began feeling more and more uncomfortable and trapped.

For some time, I had known my government job was not a good fit for me, but I couldn't quit because we needed the health insurance. During that work conference, after a couple hands-on training seminars using new technology and unfamiliar devices I could not figure out, along with yet another odd-woman-out group dinner conversation, my trapped feelings increased. I hurried back to my room and called Michael, crying. "I AM IN HELL. GET ME OUTTA HERE!"

So glad I'm not dramatic or neurotic.

I wound up putting on my big-girl pants and staying for the rest of the training. It was my job after all. However, when the survey critique came around afterward, asking if the training was useful and helpful to my job, I wrote, *No, it did not pertain in any way to my daily work.* The following year, when the training came around again, I wasn't invited to attend.

Thank God.

Other items I finally examined and acknowledged on my rape-impact list included the recurring Nazis-chasing-me-nightmare that plagued me for years, my extreme dislike of football and fraternities, the extra weight I wear to keep me invisible to men, and my powerful reaction against books and movies where innocent people are terrorized or attacked.

This time as I wrote, I did not skim or gloss over the hard parts.

I wove in the threads of the rape, no longer the-thing-that-must-not-be-named, and the effect I could now see that it had had on me—how it had been a defining moment of my life. As the words poured out, I came alive again and wrote the story I was meant to write all along. The unfamiliar depression I'd been wearing like a second sad-sack skin for so many months, finally sloughed off as my hands flew across the keyboard. And as the words flowed, my empty glass began to fill up, and when I looked in the mirror, I saw myself again.

Winston Churchill said, "Fear is a reaction. Courage is a decision." After decades of reacting in fear, I choose courage. That's why after all these years, as I watched woman after woman come forward and share their #MeToo stories of sexual assault or harassment, I finally decided to speak up as well. To share my story of the-thing-that-must-not-be-named.

And to publicly name it: RAPE.

Forty-some years ago, a group of fraternity jocks raped me on a college campus. That violation, that assault on my person —not just my vagina (a word this prissy good girl of the 1960s never used to be able to say), not just my breasts—my entire *being*, did deep, lasting damage. More than I ever realized or acknowledged. I buried my head in the sand and refused to examine or acknowledge that damage for years.

Too many years.

No longer. I now add my voice to the chorus of #MeToos.

It's time for change.

During the 2018 Golden Globes, Oprah Winfrey, in her eloquent, rousing speech, upon receiving the Cecil B. Demille Award (the first Black woman to do so), said, "Speaking your truth is the most powerful tool we all have."

Thank you, Oprah, for that important reminder.

As Twitter and Facebook exploded with women around the world sharing their sexual assault stories, one woman noted these words on a Facebook wall. "Healing started when I told…

and told again…and told again. I think trauma loses a lot of its power when it's told."

Preach.

Writing this book, speaking my truth, telling my story…has helped me heal. Finally. My prayer is that telling your story and speaking your truth will do the same for you.

It's time to let the light in.

> *It's about being alive and feisty and not sitting down*
> *and shutting up even though people would like you to.*
> —Pink

ACKNOWLEDGMENTS

This book of my soul was the hardest, most transparent, and most vulnerable book I've ever written. It began its journey nearly a decade ago as a spiritual memoir after I left fundamentalist Christianity and found my spiritual home in the Episcopal Church. Thanks to my longtime friend Cindy McCormick Coloma for suggesting I write this.

Over time, and many iterations, my "spiritual memoir" has morphed and grown into something more, thanks to the feedback and guidance of publishing pals. Thanks to Beth Jusino and Andy Meisenheimer for reading an early draft and steering me off my myriad rabbit trails and back on track.

Heartfelt gratitude to my dear friend and former editor Lonnie Hull DuPont, who gently suggested I consider adding in how my long-ago rape had impacted and affected me. It took me years before I was finally ready to examine the-thing-that-must-not-be-named and then to share it publicly within these pages, but Lonnie was right. As always. Every author needs a Lonnie in their life.

Huge thanks to my friend and agent Chip MacGregor, who loved and believed in this book from the beginning and championed it through its countless versions. (If Reese Witherspoon makes this into a movie, I'll buy you a whiskey, Chip.)

Thank you to the myriad friends and family who read this over the years (too many to list) but in particular Lisa Cook, Mary West, Dave Meurer, Shane Galloway, Ruth Kenney, and Maria Hunt. Deepest thanks to my niece Jennie for reading the section on Lexi and giving me permission to share the story of the heartbreaking loss of her beloved daughter, Alexandria Skye Damron. Sweet Lexi, you are missed every day.

A grateful shout-out to Kim Orendor for always having my editorial back.

Thanks to my photographer pal Brian Baer for taking the black-and-white photos of the myriad snapshots collected over the years.

Profound gratitude to Karen and Frank Ingram. Without your support and encouragement, this book would never have happened.

Thanks to my sweet friend and former choir director, Connie Weichert, now retired, for vetting the "Make a Joyful Noise" chapter.

Special thanks to dear clergy friends the Reverend George Foxworth and the Very Reverend Canon Mary Hauck for their kind words and spiritual insights.

Much love and gratitude to my St. Michael's Episcopal Church family.

Thanks also to Amanda Luedeke, Kate MacGregor, and The Lab Publishers for helping make this book of my soul a reality at long last.

And as always, thanks to Michael. For everything. "Shut the door."

ABOUT THE AUTHOR

Former newspaper reporter Laura Jensen Walker is the award-winning author of more than twenty books including *Thanks for the Mammogram!* and the Agatha-nominated mystery *Murder Most Sweet.*

She has appeared on hundreds of TV and radio programs across the country, including the ABC Weekend News and has given keynote addresses to women's organizations nationwide including Gilda's Club and the Susan G. Komen Foundation. Laura lives in Northern California.

To discover more about Laura and her books, please visit her website at: www.laurajensenwalker.com